D1095271

"PARADISE LOST" AND
THE XVIIth CENTURY READER

PARADISE LOST
&
The Seventeenth Century
Reader

B. RAJAN

FELLOW OF TRINITY COLLEGE
CAMBRIDGE

NEW YORK

OXFORD UNIVERSITY PRESS

1948

CONTENTS

CONTENTS

PREFACE

Most of the chapters in this book represent an attempt to see *Paradise Lost* through the eyes of Milton's contemporaries. I have tried, in other words, to reconstruct the response of an alert and qualified reader of the epic, who shared the values and interests of Milton's generation. Such a reconstruction cannot be much more than speculative, but I hope I have prevented it from becoming wholly capricious by relating it persistently to the available facts. I do not claim that the interpretation which emerges has any special status or authority; but I have found my own understanding of the epic enriched by the attempt to study it from a different viewpoint. I should add that the first chapter has little to do with this programme and that the second is merely an attempt at demolition, designed to remove obstacles rather than to reconstruct effects. The last chapter has caused me some anxiety and I hope I may be excused for not having referred to the long and indecisive debate upon its subject. I felt that I could best make my contribution by stating my own views clearly, rather than by refuting, or correcting the views of others.

With so large a subject debts are not easy to remember and I offer my apologies to those critics from whom I have learnt, and whose help I have failed to record in my footnotes. I also regret that I have not been able to make use of two volumes— Canon Hutchinson's *Milton and the English Mind* and Mr. J. S. Diekhoff's study of *Paradise Lost*—which were published while this book was in the press. A special acknowledgment is due to Dr. E. M. W. Tillyard without whose encouragement this book would never have been written. Both he and Professor Willey have very kindly read through most of the manuscript and on several occasions saved me from my ignorance. I need hardly insist on my responsibility for whatever errors remain.

CAMBRIDGE, MARCH 1947

7

MILTONIC CRITICISM:
A FOREWORD

I N order to know what a book on Milton is trying to do, it is useful to know what previous books have done. This is all the more important, not only because of the volume of Miltonic scholarship during the last thirty years, but because the trends and methods of such scholarship differ considerably from those which have prevailed in the past. I am therefore presenting a summary (which at times will degenerate into a catalogue) of those aspects of Miltonic scholarship which are specially valuable as a background to this book.[1]

It is generally agreed that Greenlaw's essay on Spenser and Milton (1917) and his later, more elaborate study of Spenser's influence on *Paradise Lost*[2] initiated a new phase in such work. Much of Greenlaw's source work is out of date but what remains permanently valuable is his insistence that Milton was a thinker as well as a poet and that, both in its assumptions and in its tendencies, his thought had much in common with the Renaissance. Similar claims had been made in 1915 by Sir H. J. C. Grierson in his article on Milton in Hastings's *Encyclopaedia of Religion and Ethics*. Their authority was still further strengthened by Professor J. H. Hanford's essay in 1919 on Milton's humanism[3] with its conclusion that Milton, far from moving away from the Renaissance, in fact moved closer to its central truths.

The next stage was to affiliate Milton's thought to those heterodox speculations, which while marginal to Renaissance thought, had sometimes acquired the status of minority traditions. Such parallelisms were usually construed to show Milton's daring and independence as a thinker. *Paradise Lost*, which the nineteenth century called "a monument

9

to dead ideas", turned out to be a mine of occult specu-
lation, materialist heresies and Kantian absolutes. Liljegren's Machiavellian portrait came in for study. Professor
Bredvold established the fact that Milton possessed a copy
of Bodin's rare and dangerous *Heptaplomeres*.[4] An article
was written on Milton's debt to Servetus, a theologian
brought to the stake by Calvin for his heresies.[5] The tendency was summed up in Professor Denis Saurat's *Milton,
Man and Thinker* (1925).[6] It continued into the thirties with
M. Larson's *Modernity of Milton*, E. C. Baldwin's work on
Semitic influences on Milton's thought, and Professor H. F.
Fletcher's two volumes on Milton's Semitic and Rabbinical
readings.[7]

Professor Nicholson's three essays on Milton, Hobbes and
More are in a somewhat different class.[8] No large claim of
influence is involved and although one may disagree on
various points of detail one cannot seriously challenge the
conclusion that Milton was alive and sensitive to the speculative issues of his time. The decade is marked too by a good
deal of indispensable spade-work: Hanford's "Chronology of
Milton's Private Studies" (1921), his work on Milton's youth
(1925), Professor A. H. Gilbert's articles on Milton's astronomy (largely but not entirely superseded by McColley's),
his *Geographical Dictionary of Milton* (1919) and E. N. S.
Thompson's essay in the same year on Milton's knowledge of
geography.[9] To these one should add Miss Langdon's mono-
graph on Milton's theory of Poetry, Miss Hartwell's work on
Milton and Lactantius, Professor J. S. Smart's still indispensable edition of the sonnets (1921), H. F. Fletcher's study
of the influence of the Bible on Milton's prose and, most
important of all, Professor R. D. Havens's monumental
survey, *The Influence of Milton on English Poetry*, which was
published in 1922.[10] Dr. E. M. W. Tillyard's *Milton* (1930)
is a comprehensive treatment of Milton's life and writing
particularly valuable for the attention it pays to the Latin
poetry and pamphlet prose as instrumental to the understanding of his development. While disagreeing on several
important matters with Saurat and Liljegren, its conclusions

are naturally greatly influenced by the scholarship of the decade which preceded it.

The emphasis throughout this decade was on Milton as a man of the Renaissance, an eclectic, an independent thinker perhaps something of an opportunist in his politics, certainly daring and original in his poetry. Professor E. E. Stoll played rather a lone hand during this period with his insistence on Milton as essentially Puritan.[11] But with the publication of Professor Haller's collection of tracts on liberty in the Puritan Revolution[12] a reaction began to set in. In the same year (1934) Professor G. C. Taylor published his study of Milton's use of Du Bartas.[13] The exaltation of Sylvester's translation to a super source can be disputed. But the second chapter presents a valuable enumeration of commonplace ideas in *Paradise Lost* which has since proved to be something of a landmark.

What happened subsequently may be subdivided as follows. First, the editing and annotating of Milton's works has continued. W. MacKellar's edition of the Latin Poems appeared in the same year (1930) as O. M. Ainsworth's edition of the Tractate on Education. Merritt Y. Hughes included the results of much recent scholarship in his edition (1935–7) of *Paradise Lost, Paradise Regained,* The Minor Poems (in chronological order) and *Samson Agonistes.* But most important of all is the Columbia edition (1931–38) of all Milton's works with Professor F. A. Patterson's invaluable two volume index. The Columbia text is the most satisfactory available, though Professor H. F. Fletcher's facsimile edition of the Poems (now in progress) demonstrates that it is by no means the last word.

Secondly, the background of Milton's controversial prose (and indeed the whole history of political ideas during the interregnum) has been investigated by such scholars as Professor Haller, Professor A. Barker, Professor A. S. P. Woodhouse, Professor W. K. Jordan, Mr. G. W. Whiting, Mr. D. M. Wolfe and Professor M. Y. Hughes.[14] Milton's essential Puritanism is firmly agreed on by these scholars; but the agreement rests on a more adequate and charitable understanding than hitherto, of Puritan thought in mid-seventeenth century England. We are beginning to understand for the first time the meaning of such terms as the "Law of Nature" and "Christian Liberty" and the part they play in the planning of *Paradise Lost*. I have tried to bring this fresh knowledge to bear on the last books of the epic and on Raphael's account of Satan's rebellion. A fuller survey is obviously called for but I leave it to those who are better equipped to provide it. In addition such research has made possible a fresh assessment of Milton's contemporary reputation which Masson has greatly overestimated.[15]

Thirdly the long argument on Milton's theology to which the principal contributors were Professor Saurat, Professor Kelley, Sir H. J. C. Grierson and Professor Sewell has been settled at last by the publication, in 1941, of Kelley's *This Great Argument*. It is clear now that *Paradise Lost* was written at the same time as the *De Doctrina Christiana* and that there are no differences of dogma between the treatise and the epic. But to say that the epic is consistent with Milton's heterodox theology is very different from saying that it implies it. I have tried to show that it need not, and was not intended to imply it, for a reader unacquainted with the "De Doctrina".

Fourthly there has been a long series of studies which cumulatively demonstrate that in its outlines and sometimes in its imagery, Milton's epic was following precedents which, by continual repetition, had acquired the status of conventions. Professor McColley's work in this field is particularly impressive, but one should also mention Arnold William's study of *Paradise Lost* and the Renaissance commentaries on *Genesis*, K. Svendsen's two articles on Milton and contemporary scientific encyclopaedias, L. B. Campbell's study of Urania as the muse of Christian Poetry, Professor A. O. Lovejoy's essay on the *felix culpa*, Professor Curry's study of Milton and the Scale of Nature, and Dr. Tillyard's incidental allusions in *The Elizabethan World Picture*.[16] The background of *Paradise Lost* is further explored in Professor Nicholson's studies of the influence of the telescope on seventeenth century imagination, in McColley's definitive examination of the sources of the dialogue between Raphael and Adam on astronomy, in

the study by E. W. Talbert and D. T. Starnes of Milton's use
of contemporary dictionaries, in G. Williamson's article on
the mortalist heresy, and in Mr. Whiting's discussion of the
background in Puritan tract literature for Belial, and of the
relation of *Paradise Lost* to contemporary travel books and
maps.[17] Since the effect of all this work is to stress Milton's
conventionality, I may add three items which strengthen this
impression: W. R. Parker's study of Greek Tragedy and
Samson Agonistes, M. Y. Hughes's account of the literary tradition which lies behind the Christ of *Paradise Regained* and last
but not least Mr. C. S. Lewis's *Preface to Paradise Lost*.[18] The
picture is not yet complete. One still has to relate *Paradise
Lost* to the ideas discussed in Hardin Craig's *The Enchanted
Glass*, Dr. Tillyard's *The Elizabethan World Picture* and
Theodore Spencer's *Shakespeare and the Nature of Man*. But the
tendency is clear and it remains to estimate its results.

Like all reactions it is likely to go too far. We have lost the
dashing diabolist of the twenties, the "thinker of terrible
thoughts", the man who, according to Saurat, "drank deeply
of the Kabbalah". We are likely to be palmed off instead with
a staid inglorious Milton, a hanger on to platitudes, a man
who says nothing unless seventeen people have said it. Both
these conceptions are untrue but their defects may perhaps
be more readily recognised if we contrast them with the nineteenth century Milton, a man whose imagination redeemed
the poverty of his intellect and whose poetry could still remain
magnificent and moving despite the barriers of an obsolete
mythology. When the nineteenth century thought of Milton
they thought of him as a poet and not as a thinker. The
thinker was merely a crabbed embittered Puritan over whom
the grand style fortunately triumphed. What was valuable
to Milton's readers was the style itself and not the doctrines
it organized, the elaborate harmonies and the recondite
allusiveness, the deep insight into unchanging human emotions. For the nineteenth century Milton's achievement was
primarily one of music and feeling; in the twentieth the interest has shifted to his ideas. What post-war scholarship has
been concerned with is the affiliations and the significance of

the beliefs in Milton's poetry and their relationship both to the life of the man and to the intellectual life of his generation.

Once this interest has been granted a further subdivision becomes possible. The best scholarship of the nineteen-twenties grew out of a belief in an intimate connection between the man and the thinker. Milton's life became the clue to his mind. His convictions, far from being the result of uncritical acceptance, or dispassionate meditation, were moulded and confirmed by the pressure of events. They took on accordingly the colouring of his character. The man was proud and iconoclastic and the thinker therefore was bizarre or original. The man converted his grievances into doctrines and the poet expressed these doctrines as mythology. Hence, in order to know what the poem was about, you had to read it as a form of autobiography, a record of what its author believed and suffered, more satisfactory than prose because you could see in it more clearly the feelings which Milton attached to his convictions. Given this bias, it was only natural that scholarship should emphasize what was personal, individual and unusual in Milton's beliefs. The thinker had been forgotten too long in the preoccupation of readers with the poet; he could not live again in the imagination of critics if his ideas were not made as colourful as his poetry. So scholarship insisted on the forbidden books which Milton read, the orthodoxies he jubilantly attacked and the strange and unnatural heresies he propounded. But when once the thinker had become the dramatic and somewhat satanic figure which critics like Saurat made of him, interest shifted insensibly to the study of his environment. Scholars now stressed what was traditional, orthodox and everyday in Milton's beliefs. His prose was valued because of his persistent and sometimes perplexed consideration of the problems which harassed Puritan England, and his poetry praised because it so ably unified what others had said on the same subject before him. This concern with Milton's political and literary background has dominated the scholarship of the last decade and interest in the *milieu* is now so ardent that there may even be some danger of our forgetting the man.

MILTONIC CRITICISM

It is fair to say then that the achievement of recent scholarship has been to call attention to Milton's beliefs and, in doing so, to remind us that we cannot dismiss the ideas in a poem as irrelevant or hostile to its poetic effect. But such a contention while true is also frustrating. It is right to insist that ideas have a function in poetry and that to ignore them, or even casually to accept them, is to destroy your perception of the poem's proportions. The difficulty lies in determining the function of these ideas, the way in which they are supposed to manipulate your emotions and the quality of assent which you are expected to bring to them. Faced with this problem I think the most helpful procedure is to suppose that the poet uses ideas in much the same way as he uses words. He uses them, that is to say, with a specially keen awareness of their history. But his using of them is itself an event in their history and though his poetry may not change the ideas themselves it does change or intensify the emotions which you bring to them. So you cannot find out what a poet is doing simply by finding out what other poets have done, since every poem is new enough for every element in it to function in a new way. And you cannot find out what the ideas in a poem mean by finding out what they have meant elsewhere to its author, for though these meanings may be unchanged, they are just as likely to be modified by the special demands which the poem makes upon them.

In such circumstances, criticism and scholarship are best employed not so much in telling us how Milton's epic was written as in suggesting how it ought to be read. The ideal critic should be also the ideal reader, and his discussion of *Paradise Lost* should be related everywhere to the effect of the poem on the audience for whom it was intended. I assume, of course, that Milton's epic was written to be read, and read by an audience with definite predilections. Some may protest that this conception is misleading, that poets write solely for the joy of writing, or in order to make themselves clearer to themselves, or to make themselves clearer to an undefined posterity. This may be true of some poets though one hopes it is not true of many. But it is not true of the poets of the Renaissance, who thought of poetry as a profession and not a therapy, and were therefore keenly and continually aware of the poet's position and responsibilities. It is certainly not true of Milton, who thought of writing a poem "doctrinal and exemplary to a nation", who wished so ardently to celebrate his country's history for his countrymen, and who even looked upon poetry as a pulpit from which truth and righteousness could be preached to his generation.

It should be conceded therefore that Milton wrote *Paradise Lost* for his time even if, in the process, he wrote it for posterity. What remains to be determined is how far that concession affects our reading of the epic and to what extent our response to it is altered by the attempt to see it through seventeenth century eyes. With some poems this difference is negligible. The emotions on which they are founded are too constant, and are too much part of human nature to vary in the minds of the generations they affect. And though the words which define them may subtly change in meaning, their qualities on such occasions can usually be inferred from the context of the experience which demands them. The nature and function of each element is made unmistakable by the whole to which it belongs. But an epic poem is seldom thus self-supporting. It is not the experience itself but a setting for experience. Its unity therefore is ceremonial rather than vital, demanding a background of co-operation and assent. So, in order to see what an epic poem is, you must see it confirming the values it assumes, and try to relate it to the background which it focuses and against which its peculiar brilliance endures. That background, let me insist, is not a personal background. An epic poem is too comprehensive and massive, too deeply concerned with its time and with its tradition, and with seeing all knowledge proportioned by its order, to be harassed, limited or drawn aside by the private implications of its author's philosophy. It may include that philosophy, or part of it, in its programme. But it cannot depart from its programme to explore it. Its public meaning is not always its private significance, and though the two may coincide in practice, in critical procedure they should be kept severely distinct.

So far, then, I have suggested that Milton's epic requires to be read against a background, and that that background is public rather than personal. It follows that, for our purposes, interest in Milton's *milieu* would be misdirected if its end were a more intimate acquaintance with the man. A poem cannot be defined genetically through its evolution in the mind of the poet. It can only be approached, as it was meant to be approached, through its effect on the audience for whom it was intended. Seen thus, the work of recent scholarship, the detailed examination of the sources of *Paradise Lost*, is useful and even indispensable. But the evidence needs to be rearranged and revalued, to be studied, not as the raw material from which the poem was built up, but as part of the equipment which the typical reader brings to it.

The question we have now to ask ourselves is: "What sort of a person was this typical reader?" This is a question which has only recently been asked of Shakespeare and hitherto it has not been asked of Milton. So one cannot turn to scholarship for an answer. But as one explores the wilderness of footnotes which scholarship has brought to the understanding of *Paradise Lost* one can hardly avoid the depressing conclusion that its would-be reader must be impossibly learned. This book, regrettably, has more than its share of footnotes and so I must hasten to add that they are regulated by a different assumption. No acquaintance with specific sources is implied. The references merely suggest the extent to which the themes discussed were part of the popular heritage and therefore accessible to the unlearned reader. I could, for instance, have extracted most of them from three books: Calvin's *Institutes*, Goodman's *The Fall of Man* and Sylvester's immensely popular translation of Du Bartas's *La Sepmaine*. But I could hardly have done so without implying that Milton was specially influenced by these authors, and I could certainly not have indicated the extent to which the same themes were utilised by authors whose allegiances may have differed considerably from those of Goodman, Calvin, or Du Bartas. My assumptions therefore are merely that Milton's audience had read books similar to these, that they were intimately familiar with the Bible, conversant with a system of divinity, and literary enough to have read a poem or pamphlet on some phase of the action of *Paradise Lost*. Moreover they could hardly have opened a tract or attended a sermon without being reminded of those great and comprehensive conceptions in which the imagination of their time was crystallized, the themes of hierarchy, order and degree, of deliverance from sin in Christian Liberty, of the second Adam dying to redeem the first and of Everyman conquering Satan on the field of Christian warfare.

Given this knowledge, the foundations would have been laid. I do not deny that readers so scantily equipped would have missed a great deal that is important in the poem, that they would have known nothing of its elaborate allusiveness, the feeling for the literature of other countries and epochs that is worked so deftly into the texture of its style. But I think that they would have seen the epic in its proper proportions and that these proportions would have been greatly different from those we impose upon the poem today. To recover these proportions is predominantly the business of this book, but the problem, I need hardly add, is too complex and intangible to be made the matter of a prefatory paragraph. What we need to insist on at this stage is the extent to which Milton's epic was accessible to the unlearned reader of his time. Erudition would have affected their feeling for the poem's nuances, for the play of light and colour on its landscapes; but it would have left unaltered their perception of its geography. Nevertheless, given this primary knowledge of the poem's architecture, the reader would have grown into familiarity with its ornaments. He would have been drawn into reading the literature massed behind it, the other poems written on its subject, the epic poems written in other languages, and encouraged to explore the controversies and problems on which so much of *Paradise Lost* is based. So learning is what the poem recommends rather than what it stipulates. Your response to it is confirmed by what you read,

and that confirmation and enrichment insensibly tempts you
to read more. Proceeding from this point of concentration to
the background of the culture which it focuses, you become
conscious of what that culture symbolized and the ultimate
values by which it was measured and justified.

So far, then, I have claimed that, given the right preoccupations and sympathies, the outlines of Milton's epic are
easily accessible and that exploration fills in rather than alters
these outlines. It follows that the intention of the poem must
be what it openly announces and that no separation not immediately obvious is possible between its real and its nominal
subject. If this were not so, your second thoughts would
qualify and not confirm your first ones. I should therefore be
inclined to dismiss from the minds of Milton's contemporaries
the sophisticated classifications made by later critics in which
the real subject becomes Paradise, or Milton, or a conflict
between reason and the passions in which Christ and Satan
are symbolic antagonists. Such interpretations may lead to
valuable results but the assumption on which they rest and
which bars our access to the seventeenth century mind is that
there is something more ultimate than the scriptures in terms
of which the scriptures need to be explained. For Milton's
contemporaries, on the contrary, the scriptures would have
been used to explain everything else. The Renaissance, whatever else it may have done, had done nothing to question this
tradition. If people read the book of nature more often, they
read it as a commentary on the book of God. If they were
enthusiastic about experimental science they applauded it
as a means of verifying religion. Their political arguments
were based on popular theology. Their theories of the social
contract began from the assumption of original sin, and their
conception of the privileges of the saints fostered their conclusions regarding the rights of man. Even scepticism started
from the premise that reason in man was obscured by Adam's
transgression and that consequently we were not to jump to
rash deductive conclusions but to sift and define the evidence
of the senses. The dogma of the fall had thus a universal
authority. Its supposition of frailty at the roots of human

nature was one which scientific evidence did not challenge and which the history of the interregnum seemed amply to confirm. Milton's contemporaries would have seen no reason for going beyond it and they would therefore have accepted as ultimate and unquestionable the Biblical argument on which his epic is founded.

That acceptance is one which brings its poetic rewards. It makes the epic representative of the deepest convictions of the civilization which produced it, true to the beliefs and temper of its time and yet true also to the tradition it fulfils. You can see what it is with the simplest of equipment; but in exploring it you acquire a European education and find the learning to which you are so pleasantly persuaded valued and set in the poetry that rewards it. So the ancient prescription is fulfilled and the speaking picture delights as it instructs. But its didacticism is something eminently civilized. It belongs to a century when poetry could still be the noblest of professions and the heroic poem the noblest of its products. Even at the end of that century Dryden could speak of the epic as "undoubtedly the greatest work which the soul of man is capable to perform".[19] An estimate as high as this carries its obligations. Those who brought to the reading of epic poetry this settled and serious conception of its stature would naturally have demanded from it the utmost which the feelings and intelligence of its time could give. "It is not sufficient", says Gabriel Harvey, "for poets to be superficial humanists: but they must be exquisite artists, & curious universal schollers."[20] So when Harvey chides Spenser for not knowing his astronomy,[21] something more is involved than a pedantic reproof. What stands committed is Ben Jonson's belief that the poet can feign a commonwealth of learning and Milton's more fervent conviction that the poet "teaching over the whole book of sanctity and vertu" must bring to that high enterprise "industrious and select reading, steddy observation, insight into all seemly and generous arts and affaires".[22] Such claims could only have been entered in an age when poetry was still the Divine Science and the Mistress Knowledge, when reality had not yet lost its poetic qualities, and when one's understanding of facts was confirmed and even completed by their appropriation in a poetic order. Few poems satisfy these ideals more amply than *Paradise Lost*. There is hardly a question which the seventeenth century could ask which it does not directly or indirectly answer. And those answers are all the more convincing because you are compelled to feel behind them the accumulated weight of the values they exemplify. There is no better justification of the Renaissance tradition that the poet should be learned, the tradition insisted on by French and Italian critics, by poets like Ben Jonson, and by scientific virtuosos like Sir Kenelm Digby.[23] Here it is in the words of an educationalist, Jan Comenius:

> Can any man be a good Naturalist, that is not seene in Metaphysicks? Or a good Moralist, who is not a Naturalist? Or a Logician, who is ignorant of reall Sciences? Or a Divine, a Lawyer, or a Physician, that is no Philosopher? Or an Oratour or Poet, who is not accomplished with them all?[24]

Milton is "accomplished with them all". What is essential in his poem would have been accessible to his unlearned contemporaries but its details and nuances would have invited them into learning. And such erudition would have been ordered and given significance by its incorporation in a poetic synthesis so ample that every field of learning seemed to imply it. So, if we must think of Milton in connection with his poetry, it is perhaps best to think of him thus, within the impersonal requirements of his office, and as possibly the last person in history to hold all human knowledge for his province.

"PARADISE LOST" AND
THE "DE DOCTRINA CHRISTIANA"

————————◦○○○○○ ❖ ○○○○○◦————————

IN considering recent Miltonic scholarship I have stressed
its persistent interest in the thinker while at the same time
criticizing the assumption that *Paradise Lost* was primarily a
vehicle for the thinker's philosophy. I suggested that the
public meaning of a poem was logically distinct from its
private significance, and should depend on the manipulation
of a common core of sentiments and beliefs which the poet
could assume in each member of his audience. Now Milton
wrote, contemporaneously with *Paradise Lost*, a highly heretical systematic theology. Until fairly recently, scholars have
been able to maintain that the beliefs which this theology
advocates are not the same as those advanced in the epic.
There was evidence (though slender evidence) for arguing
that the treatise was written before the poem, and when
further research made this contention untenable one could
still claim that the manuscript of the "De Doctrina" with
which we are familiar differed in dogma from the draft
written contemporaneously with *Paradise Lost*. But in 1941
Professor Maurice Kelley's conclusive survey of the evidence
made this theory unacceptable and most scholars now assume
that the treatise and the epic are doctrinally identical.[1] So,
unless we can point to differences in the treatment of dogma
between the two works, we will have to conclude that
Paradise Lost is primarily a vehicle for poetically expounding the
thinker's unorthodox philosophy, and that Milton values this
sort of self-expression sufficiently highly to risk making his epic
unacceptable to very large numbers of his potential audience.

In the following pages I shall try to present the evidence
which, in my opinion, makes this admission unnecessary.

My claim will be that Milton seems to go out of his way to avoid harassing the reader with his personal beliefs and that in the effort to do so he "tones down" his heresies as much as he can without becoming dishonest. But before stating the evidence for this contention I shall have to deal with the objection that there are heresies in *Paradise Lost* which do not appear in the "De Doctrina", for this, if it were true, would seriously affect my hypothesis. As far as I am aware these heresies consist of (*a*) the theory of creation by retraction, (*b*) the suspicion of Calvinism in III, 183–84, (*c*) speculations regarding the sexual nature of the creation, (*d*) the theory of latent evil in God and (*e*) the theory of an instantaneous creation. The first, second and third of these are, to my mind, untenable on the results of recent research.[2] The fourth is based on a possible misreading of "God" and anyway there is nothing calamitous in the statement that evil may be the object of God's contemplation.[3] The fifth is tenable but it is not a heresy. Its conventionality is apparent in its appearing in thinkers as diverse as Philo, Augustine, Boethius and Browne.[4] Moreover it is dramatically apt. The power of good exemplified in the "instantaneous creation" is meant to be contrasted with the laborious and eventually unavailing stratagems of evil and is part of an extended contrast between Heaven and Hell which would have been wholly acceptable to a Renaissance audience. It seems therefore that the unorthodox doctrines stated in *Paradise Lost* are all propounded in the systematic theology and accordingly the rest of this discussion will be restricted to the treatment in both works of these common heresies.

We begin with Milton's Arianism which involves us at the outset in a chaos of debate. But, keeping our eyes as far as possible on the poem, let us investigate the flux of learned commentary that swirls bewilderingly and uncertainly around it. Kelley, at the end of a comprehensive survey, maintains that *Paradise Lost* is an Arian document. Keightley finds the heresy expressed so unequivocally that "one might wonder the reader did not discern it". Barber, on the contrary, says that the poem is impeccably orthodox while

Larson maintains that it is complementary to the treatise. Sewell points to discrepancies and to hesitations and Sir Herbert Grierson provides a sort of summing up to this academic whirligig with his conclusion that "even Milton's Arianism which is fully developed in the 'De Doctrina' is not so clearly adumbrated in the poem".[5] This is very true, but what Sir Herbert Grierson does not explain is why and how this obscurity arises. Unfortunately the modern critic is in no position to do this. The Treatise comes between him and the poem compelling him to see the poem through it. To return to normal, to achieve the simplicity of response which Milton may have expected on this issue we must go back to the period, before 1825, when the Treatise was unknown. I do not say that this age is without misgivings. Toland has his doubts. Richardson points to "some conjectures" of Milton's Arianism.[6] Peignot in 1806 makes sarcastic remarks[7] and 1758 provides a formidable gesture of disapproval in the placing of *Paradise Lost* on the Catholic Index.[8] Nevertheless Newton's assertion in 1749 that "there are more express passages in this work to overthrow this opinion than any there are to confirm it"[9] was far more representative of the verdict of his time. It is possible, of course, that the eighteenth century was biased, that it was predisposed to look on Milton as orthodox, but it could not have succeeded in the attempt if there had not been evidence in the epic to support it. The nature of that evidence becomes clearer when we find that the learned Bishop, in maintaining the orthodoxy of III, 383 ff., uses precisely those proof texts which Milton employs heretically in the Treatise.[10] The discrepancy, in other words, is not in what is said, but in the things that Milton deliberately chooses to leave out.[11] He says, for instance, that the Father is manifest in the Son. But he does not add that this manifestation makes the Son inferior. He refers to the Son as receiving his attributes from the Father. But whenever he does so it is subject to the saving construction that the Son is addressing the Father, not in his divine nature, but in his mediatorial office. He versifies text after text that is quoted in the "De Doctrina" but never with the conclusions which the Treatise

24

makes them imply. When a presentation so discreetly ambiguous is set in the context of Milton's poetic achievement the result is best summed up in this doleful statement by Todd:

> The dormant suspicion of schism was unawakened while I dwelt upon the magic of his invention; and like others I was all ear only to his sweet and solemn breathing strains.[12]

Surely it is possible that what happened to Newton and to Todd is what Milton expected to happen to his readers. Collate *Paradise Lost* with the "De Doctrina" and it is Arian. It could hardly be otherwise in the nature of Milton's integrity. But read it as it was meant to be read, by itself, as an epic poem, not a systematic theology, and the heresy fades in a background of incantation. The scriptural reminiscences reverberate orthodoxy. The assimilation of image after image of encyclopaedic science and hexaemeral commentary, the pivoting of the entire action on the stock responses of Elizabethan belief, control the epic and dominate its decorum. Milton's mind is too fixed for him to succeed entirely. He cannot make his heresy irrelevant. But he tries very hard to make it incidental. He makes no denial of co-essentiality.[13] He makes only one statement that is explicitly Arian and even that has been deviously interpreted.[14] For the rest, he confounds would-be exegetes with a series of allusions which can be manipulated as evidence of Trinitarianism, Anti-Trinitarianism, a Trinity of modes or one of manifestations. But he does not wish his dogma to obtrude. It did not obtrude with Newton, or with Todd, or with that long tradition of eighteenth century imitation which took Milton as its matrix in sentiment and style. If it obtrudes on us it is because of our excessive concern with possible connections between Milton's prose and his poetry. Yet surely *Paradise Lost* should be sufficient unto itself. Our criticism needs to be subordinated to its finality. For *Paradise Lost*, as Grierson points out, is not a theological poem, and *Paradise Lost*, as Saurat points out in differing from Grierson, is a poem and not a theology. A poem is an individual entity giving "competence and confidence to the tribunal to which it appeals". Its perfection lies in its self-sufficiency. The doctrines in it can only be understood, their functions and importance can only be inferred, within the discipline which the poem sets up, a discipline which, as Milton says in another context, "is not merely the removal of disorder; but if any visible shape can be given to divine things the very visible shape and image of virtue". We are not just to poetry when we value it by the standards it rejects, or when we reduce to a theological study the work which Milton has shaped for us as "an invariable Planet of joy and felicity".

Milton's treatment of the Trinity in *Paradise Lost* is therefore entirely consistent with his unorthodox views in the Treatise. But his presentation of his heresy is sufficiently subdued to involve no challenge to the beliefs of the orthodox. However, the evidence is too dubious and too scanty for me to claim that this effect is deliberate and that it results from the exercise of of a sense of poetic proportion. I shall therefore try to corroborate my thesis by an examination of Milton's pantheism.

This is stated uncompromisingly in the Treatise:

. . . that matter I say should have existed of itself from all eternity is inconceivable. If on the contrary it did not exist from all eternity it is difficult to understand from whence it derives its origin. There remains therefore but one solution of the difficulty, for which moreover we have the authority of scripture, namely that all things are of God. . . . For the original matter of which we speak is not to be looked on as an evil and trivial thing but as intrinsically good and the chief productive stock of every subsequent good. It was a substance and derivable from no other than from the fountain of every substance . . . it merely received embellishment from the accession of forms.[15]

Observe how this is phrased in *Paradise Lost*:

Oh *Adam*, one Almightie is, from whom
All things proceed, and up to him return,
If not deprav'd from good, created all
Such to perfection, one first matter all,
Indu'd with various forms, various degrees
Of substance, and in things that live, of life;
But more refin'd, more spiritous, and pure
As neerer to him plac't or neerer tending. . . .[16]

26

These lines undeniably parallel the passage in the "De Doctrina". Nevertheless they are completely commonplace. Milton has set the stage by calling Raphael the "Wing'd Hierarch" summoning as Dr. Tillyard points out the associations of "degree".[17] What follows is merely a conglomerate of platitudes. The proposition that spirituality is increased by nearness to the divine presence is a familiar axiom of Renaissance Platonism.[18] The argument that the Universe was created from first matter has been introduced over and over again into encyclopaedias by Trinitarians and devout advocates of the Creation *ex Nihilo*.[19] The only thing that is in the slightest degree suspicious is the use of "proceed" instead of the usual "descend".[20] But such a criticism presumes an intolerable rigidity of usage. Furthermore a seventeenth century reader would have scorned to flirt with such heretical shadows. He would have recognized the conventional invocation and proceeded to register the conventional response. He would have said "Hear, hear" in reply to the Angel just as we say it in reply to a parliamentary *cliché*. Perhaps, remarking within himself that the stable boys of Bread Street could have delivered analogous homilies, he would have felt duly condescending to his ancestor Adam. The result would have been to make him feel superior rather than suspicious. Milton, we have to admit, has had the best of both worlds. He has given full satisfaction to his heretical self yet paid due deference to the feelings of his orthodox reader.

A further illustration of this tendency can be found in Milton's treatment of mortalism. Here he makes the heresy acceptable in *Paradise Lost* by stating it quite unmistakably but in circumstances which cancel its effects. The following is the relevant passage from the "De Doctrina":

> . . . previous to the entrance of sin into the world all parts of man were alike immortal; and . . . since that time in pursuance of God's denunciation all have become equally subject to death. . . . For what could be more just than that he who had sinned in his whole person should die in his whole person? Or on the other hand what could be more absurd than that the mind which is the part principally offending should escape the

threatened death; and that the body alone, to which immor-
tality was equally allotted, before death came into the world by
sin, should pay the penalty of sin by undergoing death, though
not implicated in the transgression.[21]

In *Paradise Lost* this doctrine is put into the mouth of Adam
immediately after his fall:

> . . . it was but breath
> of Life that sinn'd; what dies but what had life
> And sin? the Bodie properly hath neither.
> All of mee then shall die.[22]

The position of this passage needs to be noted with care. It
occurs after Adam's fall and before his repentance. Consequently, it can be taken to represent the product of an understanding that is both degenerate and unredeemed by grace.
Adam in other words can say what he likes and the audience
would accept it as post-lapsarian folly. Moreover this particular passage is the climax to a long and deliberately contradictory monologue, the preamble to which represents
Adam as chaos tossed "in a troubled sea of passions". After
this no Renaissance audience would have taken his conclusions seriously. Milton then is consistent to his doctrine.
But the manner of his presentation suggests that this consis-
tency is relevant only to his private satisfaction.

Yet one more example of differences in arrangement
between the Treatise and the epic can be found in Milton's
discussion of the Mosaic Law. As is well known, the "De
Doctrina" argues that the whole law is abolished by the
Gospel.

> THE GOSPEL IS THE NEW DISPENSATION OF THE COVENANT OF
> GRACE, FAR MORE EXCELLENT AND PERFECT THAN THE LAW,
> ANNOUNCED FIRST OBSCURELY BY MOSES AND THE PROPHETS,
> AFTERWARDS IN THE CLEAREST TERMS BY CHRIST HIMSELF, AND
> HIS APOSTLES AND EVANGELISTS. . . .

> On the introduction of the gospel, or new covenant through
> faith in Christ, the whole of the preceding covenant, in other
> words, the entire Mosaic Law, was abolished. . . .

> . . . the law is abolished principally on the ground of its being

DE DOCTRINA CHRISTIANA

a law of works; that it might give place to the law of grace.
. . . Now the law of works was not solely the ceremonial law
but the whole law.[23]

In *Paradise Lost* the argument is as follows:

> So Law appears imperfet, and but giv'n
> With purpose to resign them in full time
> Up to a better Cov'nant, disciplin'd
> From shadowie Types to Truth, from Flesh to Spirit,
> From imposition of strict Laws, to free
> Acceptance of large Grace, from servil Fear
> To filial, works of Law to works of Faith.[24]

To a reader unacquainted with the "De Doctrina" this
passage is merely a vigorous but conventional contrast of the
living spirit to the dead letter and of the harshness of the law
to the charity of the Gospel.[25] It says this and says it beauti-
fully; but without special knowledge you cannot assume that
it says more. The epic nowhere asserts that the whole Mosaic
Law is abolished by the Gospel. True, the wording of the
passage is compatible with such an assumption, but that is
very different from saying that it implies it. Once again
Milton is being very careful not to harass the reader with his
beliefs. The corollary may be that he is a scoundrel or a
coward, but I think it is just as likely that he has decided that
discretion is more poetic than valour.

Nevertheless the reader can protest that so far my conclusions have been anything but conclusive. All that I have
shown is that Milton's dogmas in *Paradise Lost* operate under
restraint. Cannot this restraint be explained by Milton's fear
of the personal consequences of openly stating his doctrines?
Was he not after all "In darkness and with dangers compast
round" and cannot his reticence be therefore attributed to
anxiety for himself rather than to solicitude for his reader? It
would be foolish to deny that these considerations influenced
Milton's writing, but I am not sure that they entirely explain
his treatment of Christian doctrine in the epic. For if Milton
wanted to write a poem expounding his unorthodox philosophy and was prevented from doing this by anxiety for

29

himself, one would expect two consequences to follow. First he would try not to present conjectures in the "De Doctrina" as assumptions in the action of *Paradise Lost*, and if he were compelled to do so, he would try to devise some means of distinguishing the facts in his fable from the conjectures and the fictions. Secondly, he would exercise as much as possible his right of free reasoning on things indifferent. Since on these matters he was entitled to think as he pleased he would have made quite clear exactly what he thought. Let us therefore examine some passages in *Paradise Lost* to see if this procedure is in fact adopted.

The first of these passages refers to the much discussed "begetting" of the Son which occurs after the angelic creation:

> Hear all ye Angels, Progenie of Light,
> Thrones, Dominations, Pricedoms, Vertues, Powers,
> Hear my Decree, which unrevok't shall stand.
> This day I have begot whom I declare
> My onely Son, and on this holy Hill
> Him have annointed, whom ye now behold
> At my right hand; your Head I him appoint;
> And by my Self have sworn to him shall bow
> All knees in Heav'n, and shall confess him Lord.[26]

This, as is well known, is flatly contradicted by Abdiel's reference to Christ as He

>   by whom
> As by his Word, the mighty Father made
> All things, ev'n thee, and all the Spirits of Heav'n
> By him created in thir bright degrees.[27]

This crux is resolved by Sir Herbert Grierson.

> In what sense Milton uses the word "begot" he has explained in the "De Doctrina"; "the Father is said to have begotten the Son in a double sense, the one literal with reference to the production of the Son, the other metaphorical with reference to his exaltation". . . . It is to this exaltation that Raphael refers in the scene with which the poem chronologically begins and it is this against which Satan rebels.[28]

I accept this theory, though not the Trinitarian conclusions which some commentators seem to make it imply. The passage may refer to the Son's "exaltation"; but this is no proof that He was not previously "produced".[29] But what is more important is that, despite the erudition which has been brought to bear on this passage,[30] it has only recently been noticed that there is no counterpart to this "exaltation" in the Treatise. The passage which Sir Herbert Grierson cites belongs chronologically to those events which Michael prophesies to Adam.[31] So even if we read "begot" metaphorically, and not literally, this only disposes of one half of the problem. We have still to explain why Milton uses the authority of displaced scriptural texts and the special authority of a statement by God the Father to describe an event in which there is no proof of his having believed. And if it is retorted that the poet is not tied to historical reality, that he is free to amalgamate fact with fiction in his fable, then the answer must be that this makes the fable misleading as a means of collecting and exhibiting the poet's beliefs.

It seems to me that this admission is unavoidable. Much of *Paradise Lost*, and almost all that part of it which deals with events before the Creation, is concerned with matters on which the Bible is virtually silent, and on which the "De Doctrina" has next to nothing to say. In all this vast territory there is no criterion to enable us to separate what Milton believed in from what he assumed or invented. Did he believe, for instance, in Satan's debate with Abdiel? The "De Doctrina" does not mention Abdiel. Yet surely this incident is just as much a fact within the poetry as Michael's indecisive battle with Satan in which Milton *did* believe according to the Treatise.[32] Again, on the evidence of the "De Doctrina", Milton apparently identifies Satan with Beelzebub, so that on this occasion we should be seriously wrong if we were to infer his beliefs from the arrangement of *Paradise Lost*.[33] This mixture of fact and fable, moreover, is not limited to events about which the Bible is silent; it can be found even in that part of the action for which the foundation is the Book of Genesis. Thus neither the Bible nor the "De Doctrina" have anything to say about lustful intercourse in Paradise. Yet this idea, though it is infrequent in the literature of the Fall, is insisted on by Milton in the second half of the ninth book.[34] Are we to assume that he believed in it, or did he use it only as an illustration, a speaking picture of that propensity to evil which is planted by disobedience in the minds of Adam and Eve? Again, are we to infer from the references in the ninth book to the intoxicating effects of the fruit that Milton credited the fruit with special potencies? If so, we should find ourselves in conflict with the claim of the "De Doctrina" that the act of eating the fruit was "in its own nature indifferent".[35] Finally, even in a passage as openly autobiographical as the exordium to the ninth book, Milton's remarks are not always unchallengeable. He talks for instance of the cold climate of England as inimical to his poetic genius. Yet he himself told Phillips (and Phillips subsequently told Aubrey) that "his Vein never happily flow'd but from the *Autumnal Equinoctial* to the *Vernal*".[36]

It would be tedious to continue to amass evidence of the manner in which fact, invention and conjecture are worked inextricably into the scheme of Milton's epic. Such a combination will only be disturbing to those who are concerned with Milton's poetry primarily as the embodiment of his personal beliefs. But for those who are prepared to concede that a poem has its own laws, and that every element in it contributes to its unity, the devices I have mentioned can be abundantly justified. Thus the "exaltation" sets the fable in motion.[37] But the apparently arbitrary test of obedience it enforces is analogous to that imposed on Adam and is therefore specially relevant in the sermon that is preached to him. In addition the device serves, as no alternative could have done, to illustrate dramatically Satan's pride and ambition. Abdiel is needed as an antagonist to Satan. But he is also drawn as the example Adam should follow, the image of obedience in the face of hostility, the servant of God on the field of Christian warfare. Michael's indecisive battle with Satan dramatizes the triumphant intervention of the Son. If it happens also to embody Milton's beliefs this merely means that at this point, as at others, Milton's beliefs are poetically appropriate. Similarly, the insistence on lust and intoxication in Paradise helps to drive home the aftermath of sin, a degradation made all the more inescapable by the idyllic beauty of the setting it corrupts. Finally, Milton's complaint about the English climate fits in with the accepted theory of the influence of climate on character;[38] a reference to his own method of composition would only be confusing in an exordium where the speaker is not only John Milton but also the Renaissance poet discussing the epic subject.

It is clear, then, that in deciding on the content and proportions of his epic, Milton holds himself free to supplement, moderate or modify his beliefs. His reasons for doing so are poetic rather than political; he does not consider *Paradise Lost* as a means of expounding a theological system which he would expound more openly in less dangerous circumstances. So we should not be surprised to find that Milton's beliefs are not plainly announced in his poetry even when he is considering things indifferent. In circumstances which left him free to think virtually as he pleased he still leaves us wondering exactly what he thought. I refer to his views on the location of Hell and on the date of creation of the angels. In the "De Doctrina" Milton makes it quite clear what his opinions on these matters are, though he also makes it clear that they are no more than opinions. "It is generally supposed", he admits, "that the angels were created at the same time as the visible universe and that they are comprehended under the general name of heavens." Milton points out that the opinion is "received" and held by its supporters "with more confidence than reason". He then discusses the scriptural texts which might be quoted against him, claims that "many at least of the Greek, and some of the Latin, Fathers are of opinion that angels, as being spirits, must have existed long before this material world" and concludes that "it is even probable that the apostasy which caused the expulsion of so many thousands from heaven, took place before the foundations of this world were laid".[39] Milton proceeds similarly in discussing the location of Hell. Reasons are given for the view that "Hell appears to be situated beyond the limits of this universe", the relevant scriptural texts are discussed and the support is claimed of Chrysostom, Luther and "some later divines". [40] In *Paradise Lost* there are two important changes in the treatment of this material. First, what are merely opinions in the Treatise become narrative certainties within the epic. Secondly, the argument to Book I is framed in such a manner that it suggests that these certainties may be no more than poetic assumptions and may not correspond to Milton's beliefs.

The first Book proposes first in brief the whole Subject, *Mans disobedience, and the loss thereupon of Paradise wherein he was plac't;* Then touches *the prime cause of his fall, the Serpent, or rather* Satan *in the Serpent; who revolting from God . . . was by the command of God driven out of Heaven.* . . . Which action past over, the Poem hasts into the midst of things, presenting *Satan with his Angels now fallen into Hell,* describ'd here, *not in the Center,* (for Heaven and Earth may be suppos'd as yet not made, certainly not yet accurst) *but in a place of utter darknesse, fitliest call'd* Chaos. *Here* Satan *with his Angels lying on the burning Lake, thunder struck and astonished, after a certain space recovers, as from confusion.* . . . Satan *awakens all his Legions.* . . . *To these* Satan *directs his speech, comforts them with hope yet of regaining heaven, but tells them lastly of a new World and new kind of Creature to be created, according to an ancient Prophesie or report in Heaven;* for that Angels were long before this visible Creation was the opinion of many ancient Fathers.

The importance of Milton's reticence can hardly be overstressed. For, as I have already insisted, the problems he is dealing with are matters of scriptural indifference. Upon these subjects you are entitled to think as you please. Why then is Milton so careful not to reveal what he thinks? The plea of political prudence cannot apply here and even if it did, it could not be legitimately entered since Milton's views on the angelic creation are similar to those of a royalist, Peter Heylyn. [41] So the answer must be that in violating received opinion on these subjects Milton wishes to claim a poetic justification. The question of his beliefs is never allowed to arise and all that we are required to do is to make certain suppositions for the duration of the poetry. These suppositions are given additional verisimilitude (in the Renaissance sense) by the support of "many ancient Fathers". Thus, under the most favourable circumstances, Milton's beliefs still cannot be deduced from his poetry; the conclusion can only be that it is not primarily the purpose of an epic poem to expound or exemplify the poet's beliefs.

We have now brought together sufficient evidence to make a tentative conclusion possible. In investigating the relationship between *Paradise Lost* and the *De Doctrina Christiana* we have seen that the intellectual territory they cover is the same and that, within that territory, the treatise and the epic are doctrinally identical. What varies considerably is the treatment of these doctrines. In the systematic theology they are clearly defined and outspokenly advocated. In *Paradise Lost* Milton's major unorthodoxies are presented discreetly and doubtfully, his opinions on things indifferent are never announced, and his beliefs, when they are embodied in his fable, are mixed inextricably with invention and conjecture. Some of this evidence can be dealt with by assuming that Milton was afraid to state his convictions openly; but the most satisfactory way of dealing with all of it is to assume that these differences are eventually due to differences in the media and aims of expository prose and epic poetry.

Such a conclusion would be both reasonable and adequate. It would be true to the facts and true also to the conviction that an epic poem has a validity outside the mind of its creator and the narrow resources of his personal philosophy. It is the property not of a person but of an epoch. It could never be "doctrinal and exemplary to a nation", it could never even enter the profession it accepts, if it were concerned (and since it is a poem passionately concerned) with the special and individual convictions of its author. If it is to appeal at all to the reader's sensibility, it can only do so on conditions which every reader accepts. It may be dogmatic because of the evocative power of dogma. It may argue because arguments have sometimes a poetic validity. But it can only do so by operating doctrines to which the imagina-

tion of its epoch assents, and in progressing from these doctrines to the experience of which doctrine is only a formula
and symbol. For these purposes Milton is willing to subdue
his unorthodoxies, to subordinate them to a general system of
assent, to organize his inner poetic feeling so that it issues in a
universal pattern of belief. To participate with one's readers
in a tradition and to accept that participation as a final poetic
fact, is to build creatively on the common truth which is
given and sustained by that acceptance. We will never know
Milton unless we know him as a poet. And the problem which
the poet faces is always and everywhere the same. It is to
transmit what is felt within a body of conventions and to make
those conventions work for and not against him. It is to live,
write, and aspire to thought so ardently that the commonplaces of one's time become the inner demands and symbols of
one's experience. By such successes Milton must be measured.
But a preoccupation with doctrine will not help us. All that we
can ever know of Milton's beliefs is at best an abstraction from
the poetic fact, and sometimes perhaps a distortion of that
fact, an impediment rather than a guide to understanding.

There is nothing we can rely on except the poetry. The
text is there, and our immediate business as critics is to find
out what the text meant to a seventeenth century audience.
Perhaps, as this essay suggests, it means something different to
Milton, but I do not think that these differences need concern
us. I have delineated them only to demonstrate the complexity of the relationship between Milton's beliefs and his
poetry. Granting even that this complexity is reducible to a
formula, I cannot see that it is aesthetically relevant. Furthermore, the formula depends on what you know of the poetry.
It is not a key to interpretation but its consequence. Interpretation therefore can only begin with the total response
which is given by the poetry, and it is only by a sensitive
attention to the surface of the verse that it can penetrate to
the laws of which that surface is the outcome.

Such an investigation might tell us nothing new, but at
least it would serve to put scholarship in perspective. For
scholarship tends to simplify and separate. It isolates elements

in order to see them more clearly. But in literary criticism the terms which are given by scholarship are fused in the transmuting unity of a pattern, and the totality which is thus recreated is often not predictable from its component parts. From the evidence I have cited, for instance, it is only too easy to infer that Milton *wanted* his poetry to look orthodox. But one could imply quite the opposite by studying his cosmology. There is no popular precedent for the location of Hell. There is no counterpart for Milton's top of the world with its Clapham Junction of the symbolic and the grotesque, its retractable ladder, its "inoffensive" causeway, and its periodic gales blowing Franciscans into limbo. [42] And the reason is fairly evident. Milton is not concerned with the *minutiae* of the Ptolemaic universe. He is concerned with it only for its philosophical implications of "correspondence", harmony and "degree". Consequently he can dramatize his cosmology, shape it to serve his narrative intention, and at the same time manipulate the deeper strata of belief which are evoked by allusion to the Ptolemaic scheme. His heterodoxy is usually recognizable as a poetic variation of the orthodox. Hardly ever does it imply a failure of discipline. So used, it is part of a system of persuasion, an element in an indivisible whole. The aim of criticism is to suggest this whole by analysis, and the function of scholarship is to recover and make evident those organizing assumptions, on which our perception of the whole depends.

Such an interpretation demands a new devotion to the poem, a determination not to move beyond it and a scrupulous adherence to the spirit which is its letter. It demands an access to that collective faith and bedrock of conviction, against which the splendour of poetry is set. For *Paradise Lost* is a poem born of its time. It takes what is given in everyday belief and then transforms it in its alchemy of acceptance. It is Milton's finest expression of that faith in a responsible apprenticeship to tradition which I have tried to delineate in the rest of this volume. Literary criticism has failed to record that faith. It has looked too long in *Paradise Lost* for the "Grand Style" or the sustaining period. It has sought for and criticized the music of Milton's words. But in so doing it has neglected the more elusive music of ideas, the truths which great poetry can summon into concord. Yet it is for this harmony also that *Paradise Lost* exists. Beginning then with what the verbal surface gives us, we must move to the appreciation of that richer music, which the accidents of history have corrupted and which the alliance of criticism and scholarship must restore.

"PARADISE LOST"

I

IN my previous chapter I tried to suggest some of the dangers of using Milton's systematic prose in order to elucidate his poetry. I implied that for the understanding of *Paradise Lost* we could rely on nothing except the poem itself and that therefore our immediate, though not our only business as critics, was to find out what Milton's words meant to Milton's audience. Now there are two things which you can say of a poet's audience at the outset. It has first a structure of literary expectation based on its experience of previous poetry of the kind presented. You can challenge this if you like and violate it if you dare to; but you are writing with your left hand if you choose to completely ignore it. It has secondly a structure of topical expectation, that is, it only sanctions a literary form because it serves as a vehicle for its preoccupations and for the poetic definition of the problems which obsess it.

I do not pretend of course that these sentences say one tenth of what can be said of an audience. I have written them only to suggest that there is a tradition, a literary past which a successful poem must modify and at the same time a fund of present idiom and experience which that tradition must interpret and control. It is only very rarely that a poem achieves this union. I believe that *Paradise Lost* is such a poem and in the next few pages I shall try to press this assertion home. But to keep any such demonstration within manageable limits I must refer it continually to the requirements I have outlined. I shall begin therefore with a sketch of the specific literary tradition which *Paradise Lost* inherits. Tracing the chief modifications which Milton makes to this tradition I shall attempt to show that these are poetically justifiable.

39

Finally I shall allude to the central problem of England in the Puritan Revolution, the problem of liberty without licence, and suggest there is in *Paradise Lost* a considered poetic treatment of this problem. Much as I admire Milton I will not say that he solves it. But his vocabulary is different from ours, his assumptions are fundamentally different, and at the very least the conclusions which result should help to elucidate our own.

There is now no doubt (thanks to American research which is only too often ignored) that *Paradise Lost* in its major outlines, and to a surprising extent in its detail and imagery, follows what is known as the hexaemeral genre.[1] This began as a commentary on the six days of the Creation, of which Philo's in the first century A.D. is a conspicuous early example. Something like eighty hexamerons were subsequently written by the Fathers culminating in the work of Ambrose and Basil.[2] After this the genre declined in popularity. There were of course developments from it such as the "Caedmonian Genesis" and much of the material provided by the Fathers was retained and elaborated in theological encyclopaedias, books of sentences and "Mirror Literature". But on the whole little was done to serve as precedents for Milton's epic. The mediaeval craft cycles may seem a different story. As Mr. Dustoor persuasively points out, they say a good deal that is said in *Paradise Lost*.[3] But this is not at all surprising since they begin at the beginning and end at the Day of Judgment. On closer examination the similarities are less striking than the differences. The chronology bears little resemblance to that of *Paradise Lost*. The angels are usually created on the first day and fall on the day of their creation. The conspicuous exception is the Towneley cycle where the date of the angelic creation is not clear and the fall takes place on the fifth day.[4] Usually also it is a tenth, not a third, of the heavenly host which rebels.[5] Estimates of the time taken by the fall vary from three days to forty and this gives God plenty of time to prepare Hell for their reception, Hell being part of the world and generally at its centre. Accounts of the battle in Heaven are limited to a few lines which say no more than is said in

Revelation. The literature does provide the elements of a character for Satan; but its most important function is to popularize a set of concepts to which all temporal events can be referred. After this a tradition can be assumed and much of Elizabethan literature seems to assume it.

With the Renaissance the classical hexamerons were once more made available. According to Thibaut de Maisières, the revival of interest in this genre began with the publication of Ambrose's hexameron in 1527 and Basil's in 1532, both with prefaces by Erasmus. In 1560 Avitus, Dracontius, Cyprian, Hilary and Marius Victor were brought together in a single volume.[6] Side by side with this revival came a flood of commentaries on *Genesis*. The best known of these, that of Pererius, was issued in 1590, and had run into at least seven editions by 1622. Its thirteen hundred pages were formidable enough,[7] but even this was surpassed by Mersenne's enormous and unfinished folio volume. These commentaries were pillaged by Raleigh and Browne. It is an open question whether Milton drew on them to any great extent,[8] but even if he did not, what matters is that they helped to disseminate that curious and extensive learning which is so obvious a feature of his epic. More important for our purposes, however, is the mass of epic and dramatic poetry (of which the best known example is Du Bartas's *La Sepmaine*) which grew up around this body of information. Much of this writing is intolerably tedious, and because we are unable to read it, we are only too apt to infer that it did not exist, or could have existed only as a movement of minor importance. Nothing could be further from the truth. The movement was European in its dimensions, it was founded on information which was part of the popular heritage, and it was therefore direct and powerful in its appeal, in its manipulation of the common core of sentiment which it could take for granted in each member of its audience.

So when Milton came to write his epic he did not write it on a *tabula rasa*. Behind the thunder of his great argument were massed the reverberations of a literary past. Those echoes and cadences may not have been defined but Milton caught them in a defining harmony. Before *Paradise Lost* you could exhaust yourself on the reading of innumerable hexamerons and wonder why men of genius had squandered their talents upon them. After *Paradise Lost* you saw that tradition set in order and could understand for the first time its symmetry and purpose. "Tous les *Hexamérons*", writes Thibaut de Maisières, "semblent s'unir dans une sorte de lignée généalogique pour faire éclore, après des générations d'efforts, cette oeuvre complète, qui les résume tous, qui les voue à l'oubli et qui étient leur race ayant atteint la perfection."[9] It is well said, but one must add in qualification that a work of art need not extinguish the tradition it fulfils. On the contrary it may compel us to review it. The present changes our perception of the past just as the past controls our perception of the present.

Such observations may seem too obvious to be worth recording. But it is this potency in a work of art, this ability to revise and order a tradition, this power in a great poet to be in the fullest sense critical of all that he inherits, which writers on Milton's hexaemeral affiliations ignore. There is a sense in which Professor McColley's work on the sources of *Paradise Lost* and Professor Taylor's study of Milton's use of Du Bartas are almost too successful. The very weight of the evidence which they muster, the irresistible catalogues of precedents, the authorities massed behind what seem to us casual minutiae, batter and overwhelm the reservations of the reader. Yet though such compilations are undeniably impressive it is difficult to imagine the inventive powers of Milton as surrendered wholly to conventions, however august. He is, as Professors McColley and Taylor would be the first to admit, an innovator as well as a traditionalist. But most important of all he is a poet, and to a poet the voices of tradition and revolt, of public formulae as well as of private judgments, are all subject to some certainty of insight, some poetic pattern to which they are made to conform.

To disentangle and isolate this pattern is a task always difficult and often unrewarding. We need all the evidence we can muster and a great deal which scholars might not accept as evidence. But the problem may be easier if we keep on remembering that every device adopted in a poem must have a poetic justification. The poem itself must give you satisfactory reasons for every element being what and where it is. If it accepts a tradition it is because that tradition is useful, because it helps to say what the poem is trying to assert. If it rejects it, it is because what the poem is saying cannot be said in that manner and it is worth while going against precedent to say it. The decisive evidence for Milton's intention, accordingly, should be available within the limits of the text. Corroborative evidence may sometimes be supplied by his treatment of tradition. But as we do not know enough about Milton's audience to be always certain of the traditions they may have accepted, we should be correspondingly careful in accepting this kind of evidence. Certainly, in the absence of a reasonable poetic explanation, we are not entitled to build our conclusions on it. Bearing in mind these precautions let us now turn to the argument which *Paradise Lost* proposes.

Milton's first few lines tell us about that argument. It is about man's disobedience, his fall and his subsequent redemption. In order to present this action more effectively, certain traditionally sanctioned details are introduced. The fall of the angels is used to motivate the temptation of Adam and Eve, and the creation of man is presented as a divine counter action to remedy the damage done by the fall. The material is familiar enough and I need not harass the reader with examples; but you cannot say the same of Milton's chronology. For as I have already pointed out, the opinion established during the Middle Ages, and all but universally accepted in Milton's time, was that the angels fell *during* and not *before* the creation. You can argue if you like that Milton's version was used by Caedmon and Spenser, that he had the support of several "ancient Fathers" and that Aquinas and Augustine had labelled the problem as a thing indifferent.[10] Nevertheless here is a possible departure from tradition and one should note that Milton in adopting this chronology has also made possible a certain poetic effect. You have only to look at the scheme attentively to see what it offers to any

43

competent craftsman. In the first place the action now falls into two symmetrical halves. Each half begins with a destructive action which is balanced and atoned for by a creative. The actions resemble each other sufficiently for one to make comparisons, and as it is the business of poetry to encourage such activity, it is worth while considering how it can be stimulated. Broadly speaking, we can do any, or all of three things. We can compare the creative phases in each half, or the destructive phases, or we can set up a sustained contrast between the powers of creation and destruction which runs through both halves and thereby pull them together. Milton does all three, and he does them so insistently and with such effect, that it is impossible to maintain that he does them simply by accident.[11]

A comparison between the destructive phases will help to show this. The essential difference between the angelic and human transgressions is indicated clearly at III, 93–134. Satan and his associates fall self-tempted. Man falls because he is deceived by Satan and therefore finds mercy unlike the rebel angels. This is repeated at III, 392 ff. Subject to these reservations, the common sin of Satan and Adam, the *materia prima* so to speak of evil, is disobedience. This may be manifest in many forms. In Satan it is most often displayed as an aspiration to Godhead. He revolts (I, 33 ff.) in order to equal the Most High. This is the traditional motivation and it is emphasized again at IV, 49–51, and at V, 724–26.[12] Satan's external lineaments reflect his sin. His is a "god-like imitated state", his chariot resembles that of the Son, and he sits on a hill with towers of gold and diamond which he calls "the mountain of the congregation" (II, 506 ff.; V, 760–66; VI, 99–102).[13] Eve's sin also reflects this aspiration. She is (IX, 793) "hightened as with wine". She fancies herself mature in knowledge "growing up to Godhead". Both Adam and Eve, satiated with the fruit, feel "Divinitie within them breeding wings". The motif occurs repeatedly in the ninth book. It is mentioned at III, 203 ff., and at XI, 84 ff. God the Father talks sarcastically about it.[14] All this is not to deny the importance of other elements such as Eve's unwariness and

Adam's uxoriousness. But the accumulating repetitions, the inescapable stress on a disobedience issuing in *hubris* is important because of the comparisons it enforces. You see terribly plainly that history repeats itself. You see that despite the contrasts, the varied nuances and refinements of evil, the sins of Satan, of Adam, and of Eve riot from a common stem of disobedience. There are other correspondences to hammer home this fact. In both phases obedience is claimed to an apparently arbitrary command. For Satan there is the motiveless "begetting" of the Son, for Adam the unintelligible taboo against eating the fruit. In both phases disobedience is followed by a kind of interior chaos. Satan's face is lined with passion and he feels within him "the hateful siege of contraries" (IV, 114 ff.; IX, 119 ff.). Adam is represented as tossed in a troubled sea of passions and his mind is shaken by mistrust, suspicion and discord (IX, 1121–26; X, 718). Both falls result too in lust and sexual indulgence. The intoxication of Adam and Eve with its inevitable aftermath of shame is paralleled by Satan's humiliation after his return in triumph to hell. The divinity our parents imagine they feel within them is burlesqued ruthlessly by Sin and Death (IX, 1008–11; X, 243 ff.). In citing these similarities I do not wish to argue that the destructive phases in both halves are identical. This is patently untrue. But what can be argued is that the differences rest on an underlying sameness which is part and parcel of what Milton has to say and that the symmetry of his plot is an indirect way of saying it.

The similarities between the creative phases are less numerous. The basis of the comparison is the *felix culpa* which, by Milton's time, had become a poetic commonplace.[15] Strictly speaking this should apply only to the Fall which is good in so far as it occasions the Atonement. But Adam, in speaking of it (XII, 469 ff.) also makes a specific comparison of the Creation to the Atonement. The supporting paradox of good from evil is a familiar feature of the epic. Satan (I, 157 ff.) sees it as characteristic of God's providence,[16] and a little further on it is made a feature of the Archangel's punishment that his malice serves only to assert God's goodness. These

45

passages should be sufficient to compel a comparison of the
Creation to the Atonement, but to make matters certain the
motif is used twice in the seventh book. It is included in the
hymn (182 ff.) which is sung before the Son journeys out into
Chaos and it is part of the celebrations (613 ff.) which take
place on His triumphant return. The comparison is further
strengthened by the fact that the minds of Adam and Eve
when fallen (IX, 1121 ff.) are described in imagery reminiscent of that of Chaos, and by the events of the tenth book
which, as I shall subsequently indicate, is a cosmic expansion
of this inner, mental catastrophe. The result of this lapse into
Chaos is that the Atonement can be more effectively presented as a second Creation, thereby reinforcing the correspondences I have cited.

The similarities between the creative and destructive
powers can be considered under two headings. First there is
a set based on the traditional comparison of Christ to
Adam.[17] Milton alludes to this at I, 4–5 and more explicitly
at XI, 382–84. At V, 384–87 and at X, 133 he strengthens
the association by comparing Mary to Eve.[18] But more
important than any of these is III, 285 ff. where an elaborate
and highly effective comparison is made between Adam's fall
and Christ's atonement. The biblical imagery which dominates this comparison would have helped to stamp it on the
minds of Milton's audience.[19] But it is also emphasized by
being interwoven with a far more complex series of correspondences, namely those worked out between the powers of
Heaven and Hell. Here the material is so rich that it is
difficult to know where to begin, but perhaps the most
striking likenesses and differences are those between the
councils of Book II and Book III. In both councils important
decisions are taken. The one in Hell initiates the destructive
action which is central to the poem, the one in Heaven is told
of the Atonement which alone can redeem it. Volunteers are
invited. There is silence in Heaven as in Hell. Both Satan and
Christ offer themselves for the opposing enterprises, but the
one speaks distended by "monarchal pride", the other in the
fullness of charity and love. The angels bow "lowly reverent"

46

to the Son and bend towards Satan "with awful reverence prone". The "deafening shout" which marks the dispersal of the infernal council is contrasted with the shout "Loud as from numbers without number, sweet" with which the heavenly conclave ends. The diverse occupations of the fallen angels can be opposed to the hymn of praise which is sung by all in Heaven. Hardly less striking are the resemblances between the Creation and the building of the causeway from Hell as it is described in the tenth book. Christ comes forth into Chaos from the gates of Heaven. Sin and Death issue from the gates of Hell. They brood over the waters in a way reminiscent of the Holy Spirit. But whereas the Son creates through the power of His word, Sin and Death are compelled to make do with substitutes: Gorgonian rigour and asphaltic slime. The finished causeway, "Smooth, easie, inoffensive down to Hell" may be compared to that "broad and ample rode, whose dust is Gold" which leads through Heaven to the house of God.

Mention of this should remind us of something which is no whit less ingenious. I refer of course to Pandemonium which is constructed with amazing rapidity by Mammon and Mulciber. Surely it is no accident that the *roof* of Pande-monium is made of the same material as the *pavement* of Heaven. The gates of Hell too flying open with "impetuous recoile and jarring sound" are meant to be contrasted with their heavenly counterparts (II, 879–83; VII, 205–9). Similarly, while the imperial ensign unfurled by Azazel is emblazoned with "Seraphic arms and Trophies", those advanced in Heaven are emblazoned with "Holy Memorials, acts of Zeale and Love" (I, 536–40; V, 588–94). Finally there are a series of resemblances between the Father and the Son and Satan. I have already mentioned the latter's chariot, the mount on which he is "exalted", and the fact that both Christ and he are raised to their Stations through merit. In addition the Father's delegation of His powers to the Son is paralleled by Satan's sending Sin and Death to earth as his viceregents (III, 317–20; V, 606–11; X, 403–5). Again, the Son sits beside the Father "in bliss imbosom'd", while Sin

47

looks forward to sitting at Satan's right hand, "Thy daughter and thy darling without end" (V, 597; II, 866–70). The implications behind these parallels vary. Sometimes we are merely reminded that the fallen angels retain the dignities which were theirs in Heaven. At other times the resemblances are scarred by savage burlesque. Yet this too is the result of Satan's governing obsession—"Evil be thou my good". It is this which makes Hell a perverted creation and which ensures that so much that is done in Heaven is jeered at and parodied in Hell. To understand this is to penetrate to the heart of the epic, to seize on that massive and symbolic symmetry to which *Paradise Lost* was intended to conform.

It should be clear from this list of correspondences not only that they bulk large in the epic, but also that they play an important part in establishing and stressing the symmetry of its action. Yet they are used relatively seldom in hexaemeral literature. And when they are used frequently, as in Giles Fletcher's longer poems, they are only used to enforce a rhetorical comparison. It is therefore Milton's peculiar achievement to have employed them en masse and yet to have built them into the architecture of his epic, an architecture all the more satisfying because it is so just to the nature of its material.

The likelihood that such correspondences are more than mere embellishments is also confirmed by some of the other departures from tradition which are made in *Paradise Lost*. Thus, in the battle in Heaven, Milton represents Christ as triumphing over Satan after Michael and Satan had waged an indecisive conflict, when most of his contemporaries would have identified Michael with Christ.[20] He could have argued that this version was not unorthodox and that it was used in the *De Victoria Verbi Dei* of the Catholic bishop Rupertus Tutiensus.[21] But I think he would also have suggested that in thus dramatizing Christ's intervention, he intended to contrast the power of good with the comparative impotence of evil. It is in this spirit that Christ's miraculous journey into Chaos is set against Satan's difficult and hazardous voyage through it. His act of creation "more swift than time or

motion" is meant to contrast with Satan's laborious stratagems. Finally, Christ's triumph in Heaven is poised against
His triumph on the cross. The one is shown in the panoply of
military conquest, the other as a battle waged and won in
the mind which, while less spectacular, is in no way less
effective.

Even more to my purpose, however, is the preliminary
temptation in the fourth book. This occurs nowhere else in
the range of hexaemeral literature. If it had occurred Professor McColley would have found it. But he has not found it
and as a result he is forced to talk of confusions, lack of
agreement, and ambiguities in the tradition which Milton
is supposed to be exploiting. Briefly, Professor McColley
claims that there was a divergence of opinion regarding the
date of Adam's fall. Most commentators believed that he fell
on the first day of his creation, but a strong minority believed
that he fell a week later. Milton tries to have the best of both
worlds by assigning a tentative temptation to the first day,
and the second, successful temptation to the eighth.[22] It is an
ingenious account but I find it unacceptable. The chronology
on which it is based is highly dubious[23] and I cannot see what
Milton is supposed to be achieving poetically by appealing
to the dual tradition which Professor McColley postulates.
Moreover only a very erudite and sophisticated reader could
have recognized that such an appeal was being made. Finally,
the device involves Milton in serious difficulties. He has to
find something for Satan to do between the temptations, and
the best he can do is to make him wander seven times round
the earth, thereby giving Newton his chance to write a
learned footnote. However, several poetic reasons can be
cited for this procedure, and all of them seem to me more
convincing than those put forward by Professor McColley.
Eve's dream is effective as an omen, it involves a deft use of
supernatural machinery, and besides providing a pretext for
a discussion on faculty psychology, it makes possible an
encounter between Gabriel and Satan which no reader of
Milton would like to see omitted. But what is most important
for my purpose is that the actual temptation is anticipated in

49

Eve's dream with a detail that is all the more rewarding given the system of correspondences I have outlined.[24] Thus, the appeal to Eve's vanity and Satan's claim that the fruit makes one god-like are common to both episodes. Again, in the ninth book it is the smell of the fruit which finally persuades Eve to taste it. So also in recounting her dream she says:

> ... the pleasant savourie smell
> So quick'nd appetite, that I, methought,
> Could not but taste.

The results of eating the fruit are also similar. Adam and Eve in the ninth book feel "Divinitie within them breeding wings / Wherewith to scorn the Earth". This immediately recalls the last phase of Eve's dream.

> Forthwith up to the Clouds
> With him I flew, and underneath beheld
> The Earth outstrecht immense, a prospect wide
> And various.

If the reader feels that these resemblances are trivial, I could refer him to the building of the causeway from Hell to the top of the world in the tenth book of the epic. Here again there is no precedent for the incident in the literature of the Temptation. You can treat it as an eruption of that grim and semi-private sense of humour which runs riot so depressingly in Limbo, or treat it as an innovation deliberately introduced in accordance with the correspondences I have outlined. Again the Sin-Death allegory may be no more than an elaboration of material in Spenser and Fletcher. But with Satan, Sin and Death make a kind of infernal Trinity and the contrast of this with its heavenly counterpart can be defended, even if its results are often not poetically justifiable.

In thus interpreting some of Milton's departures from the hexaemeral tradition, I do not wish to imply that all his innovations should be treated on this basis. Sometimes— Satan's journey through Chaos is an example—his devices need no justification beyond the poetry they make possible. At other times what strikes us as a failure may be traced to the intrusion of a private and irrelevant emotion. Sometimes

the cross references I cite may account for only a part of
Milton's intention and at other times they may account for
nothing at all. I do not deny these alternatives, but I should
like to emphasize that, as far as I am aware, nothing that
Milton does is incompatible with my hypothesis, and that
many of the events in his epic gain in richness if we agree to
locate them within this symbolic pattern of repetition and
recurrence.

This brings me to what I hope is my firmest argument for
the interpretation I am proposing. It seems to me that what
matters in a literary "explanation" is not so much its consis-
tency with the facts—there are other explanations which fit
the facts as well and for some readers fit them more readily—
as the standard of poetic achievement it implies. It is possible
to maintain that the contrast between the Creation and the
building of the Causeway from Hell is inconclusive, that
there are precedents for Eve's dream in the classical epic, and
that Milton's unconventional chronology and unconventional
treatment of the battle in Heaven prove only that he is presenting the theology of the "De Doctrina" in the poetic
trappings of *Paradise Lost*. But an explanation of this kind is
really a disguised apology. You cannot justify an event in
Paradise Lost by pointing out that it is sanctioned by a systematic theology, even if it is Milton's, or a classical epic,
even if it is Homer's. The reasons you seek should be poetic
reasons and Milton's borrowings, alike from tradition and
his own bizarre beliefs, should be inexorably related to some
poetic plan. That plan I have tried to discover in the massive
contrasts between creation and destruction and in all the
more delicate resemblances of detail which the correspondences developed in the epic imply. Much that Milton accepts
in the hexaemeral tradition, much that he ignores and much
that he obviously violates is justified and ordered by this
symmetry. And to certain minds it is important that it is so
justified. For there are those to whom symmetry is a token of
ultimate order, for whom discipline remains "the shape and
image of virtue" and not merely an unavoidable and harassing restraint. To such men—and there were many such in

Milton's England—there would have been an aesthetic satisfaction in contrasting Hell with Heaven and in finding the temptation anticipated in Eve's dream. The sustained massing of comparison and contrast, the moral enrichment of every theme by its analogue, would have helped to typify, for them, that struggle of light with darkness which the Providence of God administers in history.

In writing for such people moreover, Milton had one very formidable asset at his disposal. I refer to that system of comparison and intricate analogy which is so characteristic of the Elizabethan outlook. Hitherto I have avoided discussing the use of this system in *Paradise Lost*, and limited myself to those correspondences which are specific to the epic and do not exist apart from the events which they integrate. But if Milton meant such correspondences to be more than merely decorative, the odds are that he would have reinforced them with analogies which were not peculiar to his argument, and which were part and parcel of the seventeenth century mind. The two sets would then have drawn attention to each other because of their proximity, and together they would have encouraged a certain way of looking at the epic. I think that this method yields valuable results and so in the rest of this chapter I shall try to apply it to our understanding of *Paradise Lost*. But before doing so I shall have to digress, not into an account of the conventions themselves—these have been studied elsewhere and the essays are easily accessible— but into an outline, however unsatisfactory, of the emotional commitments which such beliefs imply.

II

Dr. Tillyard points out in *The Elizabethan World Picture* that "the Elizabethans pictured the universal order under three main forms: a chain, a series of corresponding planes and a dance".[1] I do not propose to discuss here the elaborate and often fascinating refinements of detail which lay behind

these figures. What I want to insist on is their interconnec-
tion. It is easy, and it is fatal, to regard these metaphors
simply as queer conceits, ornamental bric-à-brac, or the
furious mouthings of libidinous poetasters. Nothing could be
further from the truth. The "Great Chain", as Professor
Lovejoy's now classic study[2] demonstrates, arose from the
attempt to prove that the world God created was the best of
all possible worlds. The correspondences symbolize the
settled and serious belief that all orders reflect a universal
order. The dance exhibits that order in perfect motion. And
taken together the metaphors stand for a conviction which is
not expressed by any of them singly. You need the Great
Chain to signify the bewildering variety of God's creation.
You need the correspondences to assure you of its underlying
sameness. You need the dance to suggest the union of ecstasy
with control, the underlying discipline which animates the
universe. No one word can stand for all these qualities. But
for those who want one word solutions, I suggest that the
word should be "harmony". For harmony suggests a correspondence which is not an identity, a music which is more than
the separate notes which make it, a whole to which each
element mysteriously contributes and which the arbitrary
assertion of any element destroys. Perhaps that is why no
Elizabethan could talk of order without mentioning harmony.
"A publike weale", says Elyot, "is made of an ordre of
estates and degrees and by reason thereof, containeth in it a
perfect harmony."[3] Hooker, more eloquently, says much the
same thing of law: "Her seat is the bosom of God, her voice
the harmony of the world; all things in heaven and earth do
her homage."[4] Dryden talks of the "universal frame" beginning from harmony; Shakespeare of discord when the string
of degree is untuned, and Milton of "disproportion'd Sin"
jarring against "Nature's Chime". Isidore of Seville says
categorically: "Nothing exists without music; for the universe
itself is said to have been framed by a kind of harmony of
sounds, and the heaven itself revolves under the tones of that
harmony."[5] But the feeling behind such remarks is perhaps
best expressed in this quotation from Bishop Reynolds:

. . . as God is in his Temple, the Church, So is He in his Pallace, (if I may so call it) the World, a God of Order, disposing every thing in Number, Weight, and Measure, so sweetly as that all is harmonious, (from which harmonie, the Philosophers have concluded a Divine Providence) and so powerfully, as that all things depend on his Government, without violence, breach, or variation.

And this Order and Wisdom, is seene chiefly in that sweet subordination of things each to other, and happie inclination of all to their particular ends, till all be reduced finally unto Him, who is the Fountaine, whence issue all the streams of their limited being, and the fulnesse of which all his creatures have received.[6]

But perhaps the most elaborate discussion of this "music of order" is in a neglected passage from Cowley's *Davideis*. This deserves to be treated as a *locus classicus*, not only as a description of the Creation, but because in employing the metaphors of music it invokes both the traditional comparison of the macrocosm to the microcosm, and the traditional symbol of the dance:

> As first a various unform'd *Hint* we find
> Rise in some god-like *Poets* fertile *Mind*,
> Till all the parts and words their places take,
> And with just marches *verse* and *musick* make;
> Such was *Gods Poem*, this *Worlds* new *Essay*;
> So wild and rude in its first draught it lay;
> Th'ungovern'd parts no *Correspondence* knew,
> An artless *war* from thwarting *Motions* grew;
> Till they to *Number* and fixt Rules were brought
> By the *eternal Minds Poetique Thought*.
> *Water* and *Air* he for the *Tenor* chose,
> *Earth* made the *Base*, the *Treble Flame* arose,
> To th'active *Moon* a quick brisk stroke he gave,
> To *Saturns string* a touch more soft and grave,
> The *motions Strait*, and *Round*, and *Swift*, and *Slow*,
> And *Short*, and *Long*, were mixt and woven so,
> Did in such artful *Figures* smoothly fall,
> As made this decent measur'd *Dance* of *All*.

> In this *Great World* so much of it we see;
> The *Lesser, Man,* is all o're *Harmonie*
> Storehouse of all *Proportions, single Quire*
> Which first *Gods Breath* did tunefully inspire.

Other illustrations could be cited but it seems to me useless to multiply examples which point unanimously to the same conviction. Behind them all lies the recurrent and indelible belief that the nature of all things is fulfilled in the universal pattern they create and sustain. There is a "one right discipline" for the Universe as well as the Church. There is an eternal order within which all things exist and outside which they are doomed to self-destruction. The obligations implied by such an order are summed up in what Mr. C. S. Lewis calls the hierarchical conception:

> According to this conception degrees of value are objectively present in the universe. Everything except God has some natural superior; everything except unformed matter has some natural inferior. The goodness, happiness and dignity of every being, consist in obeying its natural superior and ruling its natural inferiors. When it fails in either part of this twofold task we have disease or monstrosity in the scheme of things until the peccant body is either destroyed or corrected. One or the other it will certainly be; for by stepping out of its place in the system (whether it step up like a rebellious angel or down like an uxorious husband) it has made the very nature of things its enemy. It cannot succeed.[7]

The inequalities assumed in this scheme of obligations are emphasized, among others, by Elyot:

> every kynde of trees, herbes, birdes, beastis and fishes besyde their diversity of formes have (as who sayth) a peculiar disposition appropried unto them by God theyr creatour: so that in every thyng is ordre, and without ordre may be nothing stable or permanent; and it may not be called ordre, except it do contayne in it degrees, high and base, accordynge to the merit or estimation of the thyng that is ordred.[8]

To this we may add the following from Fortescue:

God created as many different kinds of things as he did creatures, so that there is no creature which does not differ in some respect from all other creatures and by which it is in some respect superior or inferior to all the rest. So that from the highest angel down to the lowest of his kind there is absolutely not found an angel that has not a superior and inferior; nor from man down to the meanest worm is there any creature which is not in some respect superior to one creature and inferior to another, so that there is nothing which the bond of order does not embrace.[9]

Now what is revealing in these quotations is that it never occurs to Elyot or Fortescue that order can possibly be separated from degree. Every created thing must have a superior and an inferior. If this is not so, the alternative is chaos. Hence it follows that the sin above all sins, the sin which opened the flood gates to disaster, is the violation and denial of degree. Mercator puts the matter perfectly for our purposes:

> Seeing then they were most wisely created for the use and service of man, as well in the superiour as in the inferiour world, what a faire harmony was there then? When the lower things did accord with the highest; and expected help from them; and the highest communicated their gifts to the lowest, and all things served man until he should be translated of God into his heavenly habitation. This correspondencie, this beautie of State had continued inviolable if Adam had not sinned. . . .[10]

The passage brings together a series of important though everyday ideas. It emphasizes the concord, the unity behind all creation. It stresses the obligations of obedience and sovereignty which each being owes to the beings above and below it. It mentions the Renaissance commonplace of man's overlordship of the visible creation[11] and the equally familiar belief that man, placed on earth, could work his way up to heaven.[12] Finally it refers to Adam's sin as a violation of "correspondencie", a return to the chaos "where degree is suffocate". There are several ways in which this violation can be presented. You can follow the book of homilies and identify it with revolt. You can follow the political theorists and attempt to relate it to the Law of Nature. But to a poet in the early seventeenth century, the obvious choice would have been to treat it in terms of faculty psychology, and to interpret the Fall as a surrender of reason to the passions. The version was one which no one would have disputed and was independent of any political programme. Furthermore the apparatus of comparison and analogy to which it referred could be taken for granted with the typical reader. Jacobean dramatists had made its exploitation a fine art. Books on the subject like La Primaudaye's *French Academy* were running into several editions. Poems had been written on the anatomy of the soul, ranging from Davies's delightful *Nosce Teipsum* to Phineas Fletcher's unreadable *Purple Island*. Finally, the dramatic possibilities of the subject were immense. To set this seemingly inconsequential act against the cosmos which its wilfulness depraved, to involve the whole machinery of correspondences in the endless terrible logic of catastrophe, to refine, eke out and attenuate disaster to the brink of that chaos where Christ's atonement redeemed it, to do all this in terms of a symbolism rooted and enveloped in popular feeling —these surely were opportunities which no poet worthy of the occasion could ignore.

Milton of course does not ignore them. He treats the Fall as a usurpation of reason by appetite. Rebellion in the soul leads to disorder in the cosmos as well as to chaos in the body politic. The stock correspondences between the soul, the macrocosm, and the State, are used to expand the dimensions of the catastrophe, but they are also linked structurally to the correspondences I have mentioned in my first section. The two sets consequently draw attention to each other and jointly illuminate what Milton has to say. This amalgamation of the hexaemeral tradition with the symbolism associated with degree is, of course, not unprecedented. But *Paradise Lost* combines the elements so deftly that it helps to define the essential nature of each.

However, against any such hypothesis, one very deadly objection can be urged. It is true that the symbolism Milton employed fits aptly and inevitably into the pattern of his epic. It is true that the importance of that symbolism, its emotional impact on the Elizabethan mind, is only now being recognized and assessed. But Milton wrote *Paradise Lost* after the civil war and we can argue that audiences were no longer interested in the conception of order which I take to lie behind it. The Mediaeval synthesis was giving way to the Newtonian. The correspondences which typified that synthesis had already fallen so much into disuse that they occur very rarely even in the voluminous literature of the interregnum. By 1697 Swift could satirize them in *A Tale of a Tub*[13] and Johnson eighty years later, discussing a commonplace comparison of the macrocosm with the microcosm, described the simile as "abstruse and profound".[14] Addison makes mistakes about Milton's cosmology[15] and is sufficiently ill-read to maintain that the walls of the Ptolemaic universe were shattered by Descartes.[16] Pope presents the Chain of Being, not as a means of ascent to God, but as an argument for necessitarian optimism and the placid assertion that whatever is is right. Even in 1670, only three years after the publication of *Paradise Lost*, John Eachard could inform the clergy that "he that has got a set of similitudes calculated according to the old philosophy and Ptolemy's system of the world, must burn his commonplace book and go a gleaning for new ones".[17] If Milton chose to revive a symbolism so evidently dying, we must assume that he did so for a cultivated minority, that his epic was written for "fit audience though few". What then becomes of his earlier resolution to write a poem "doctrinal and exemplary to a nation", a unifying and permanent embodiment of the consciousness and culture of his age?

I have raised the problem in this way because I do not think it insoluble. There are times when a man can only preach effectively by preaching in the wilderness. It is probable that John Milton was such a person and that Restoration England was for him such a period. But the answer goes deeper than this kind of opposition. The power of a great writer to order a tradition, to endow it with some kind of retrospective logic, is among the chief forces which keep traditions alive. And the tradition which *Paradise Lost* attempts to keep in being, the massive, unchallengeable synthesis of knowledge it asserts, is one far richer and far more reassuring than the fragile, limited substitutes which have replaced it. As long as the effort to preserve it could be made, it was the business of a responsible poet to make it. Milton made his effort too late to be completely successful. But to say that he did not do everything is not equivalent to saying he could have done more. The conventions he used may have begun to disintegrate but their reinforcement by the pattern of the poem, the emotions they help to define, and the problems they obliquely illuminate contribute, I feel, to a richness and validity which no alternative system could have yielded. It required both honesty and unusual courage to think with such strength in so uneasy an interim. And even those who are not interested in the functions of such honesty, or in the deserts of controversy which bred it, are nevertheless compelled by it to be more fully conscious of the tradition it revives and the settled assurance which is its poetic outcome.

III

It will be remembered that after the first and unsuccessful temptation Raphael is sent down to earth to instruct Adam in the ways of righteousness. Why he should need to do so is not clear. For Adam, according to Purchas, was the greatest philosopher that "ever the earth bare".[1] According to Augustine "his mental powers surpassed that of the most brilliant philosopher as much as the speed of a bird surpasses that of a tortoise".[2] Moreover he has already given us an indication of his learning by lecturing to Eve on faculty psychology.[3] Nevertheless the angel is sent down to instruct him and is invited to dinner by Adam, who ventures to doubt if the food is satisfactory. Raphael reassures him. Everything that is created needs to be sustained and fed, just as the grosser elements in the universe feed the purer.[4] Having finished these adumbrations of the hierarchic principle the angel falls to his viands "with keen dispatch / Of real hunger and concoctive heat".[5]

The meal is rounded off with liquor, but this evidently proves harmless in the state of innocence. As the occasion demands an after-dinner speech, Adam asks the appropriate leading question and the angel, with no more ado, delivers his homily on the Scale of Nature:

> O *Adam,* one Almightie is, from whom
> All things proceed, and up to him return,
> If not deprav'd from good, created all
> Such to perfection, one first matter all,
> Indu'd with various forms, various degrees
> Of substance, and in things that live, of life;
> But more refin'd, more spiritous and pure
> As neerer to him plac't or neerer tending
> Each in thir several active Sphears assign'd,
> Till body up to spirit work, in bounds
> Proportiond to each kind. So from the root
> Springs lighter the green stalk, from thence the leaves
> More aerie, last the bright consummate floure
> Spirits odorous breathes: flours and thir fruit
> Mans nourishment, by gradual scale sublim'd
> To vital Spirits aspire, to animal,
> To intellectual, give both life and sense
> Fansie and understanding, whence the Soule
> Reason receives, and reason is her being,
> Discursive or Intuitive; discourse
> Is oftest yours, the latter most is ours,
> Differing but in degree, of kind the same.
> Wonder not then, what God for you saw good
> If I refuse not, but convert, as you,
> To proper substance, time may come when men
> With Angels may participate, and find
> No inconvenient Diet, nor too light Fare:
> And from these corporal nutriments perhaps
> Your bodies may at last turn all to Spirit,
> Improv'd by tract of time, and wingd ascend
> Ethereal, as wee, or may at choice
> Here or in Heav'nly Paradises dwell;
> If ye be found obedient, and retain
> Unalterably firm his love entire
> Whose progenie you are.

The best way to understand this passage is to read it as an academic exercise on degree. This is seldom done by critics, who either delve in it for occult information or talk condescendingly about its quaintness. I have tried to answer the charge of unorthodoxy elsewhere. It remains to be added that Milton's assumptions, whether quaint or not, are endemic to the seventeenth century mind and have to be taken as our terms of reference. When we do this we can perhaps appreciate better the skill with which these assumptions are related. Milton first asserts that the whole creation proceeds from one first matter, that each created thing has its place and function, and that created things are more spirituous and pure in proportion as they are nearer to God. Differences between them, arc of degree and not of kind. Thus, the vegetable creation culminates in fruits and the "bright consummate floure", but these in turn form the basis of man's diet and are thereby converted into vital, animal, and intellectual spirits. Milton is here alluding to the everyday theory that the spirits arose from the conversion of food to blood in the liver. As Burton puts it:

Spirit is a most subtle vapour which is expressed from the blood, and the instrument of the soul, to perform all his actions; . . . of these spirits there be three kinds according to the three principal parts, brain, heart, liver; natural, vital, animal. The natural are begotten in the liver and thence dispersed through the veins, to perform those natural actions. The vital spirits are made in the heart of [i.e. from] the natural, which by the arteries are transported to all the other parts: if the spirits cease, then life ceaseth as in a syncope or swooning. The animal spirits formed of the vital, brought up to the brain, and diffused by the nerves to the subordinate members, give sense and motion to all.[6]

Milton departs from Burton by leaving out natural spirits, and adding intellectual spirits, which I think are his invention. But he is quite conventional in his insistence that these spirits are the executives of the soul, that sense, fancy, and reason itself, are powerless without them.[7] This insistence on the continuity between the animate and inanimate, naturally suggests that body may work up to spirit and that man can be "improv'd" into an angel. There is nothing that is at all unusual about these conceptions and the suggestion that man may be transformed into an angel makes it all the more tragic that he elects to be a beast. The promise however is linked to a condition—"if ye be found obedient".[8] Disobedience hereafter becomes synonymous with the violation of "degree". The forthright statement of the basis of order provides a standard by which all defections should be judged. Adam recognizes this easily enough. He congratulates the angel on his exposition of the Scale of Nature, confirms that one can ascend to God "through contemplation of created things", and asks what Raphael means by his warning to be obedient.[9] The angel, after touching on free-will, proceeds to instruct Adam in celestial history. Now the fact that the account of Satan's revolt and the Creation is made to follow a text-book exposition of the Scale of Nature implies that a connection is meant to exist between them, and the implication is confirmed by Raphael's repeated allusions to the symbols of "degree". Thus at V, 574–6 a correspondence is hinted at between earth and heaven. Forty lines later the cosmic dance is made an analogue of the celestial.[10]

> That day, as other solem dayes, they spent
> In song and dance about the sacred Hill,
> Mystical dance, which yonder starrie Spheare
> Of Planets and of fixt in all her Wheeles
> Resembles nearest, mazes intricate,
> Eccentric, intervolv'd, yet regular
> Then most, when most irregular they seem,
> And in thir motions harmonie Divine
> So smooths her charming tones, that Gods own ear
> Listens delighted.

There is a suggestion, but no more than a suggestion, that the music of the spheres too may have its heavenly counterpart. But, in the end, it is the poetry itself, the audacious combination of the elaborate and spontaneous which makes us accept the order which it celebrates. Milton has said many things which are more spectacular. But he has never said anything which is more inevitable. That gaiety, innate yet ceremonial, those turning, pirouetting half rhymes and caesuras, reach to the heart of what discipline can give us. Milton's craft is not always as consummate. But he continues to play on the evocations of degree by references to Satan's "hierarchal standard" and to triple hierarchies of angels,[11] reaching an ironical climax in Satan's treatment of the Son's exaltation as a violation of the hierarchical principle:

> Will ye submit your necks, and chuse to bend
> The supple knee? ye will not, if I trust
> To know ye right, or if ye know your selves
> Natives and Sons of Heav'n possest before
> By none, and if not equal all, yet free,
> Equally free; for Orders and Degrees
> Jarr not with liberty, but well consist.
> Who can in reason then or right assume
> Monarchie over such as live by right
> His equals . . . ?

The argument is all the more interesting because it is a perfectly orthodox version of the claim that monarchy is not grounded on the law of Nature. Here, for instance, is a quotation to the same effect from Rutherford's *Lex Rex*:

> . . . princedom, empire, kingdom, or jurisdiction hath its rise from a positive and secondary law of nations, and not from the law of pure nature. The law saith, there is no law of nature agreeing to all living creatures for superiority; for by no reason in nature hath a boar dominion over a boar, a lion over a lion, a dragon over a dragon, a bull over a bull. And if all men be born equally free (as I hope to prove) there is no reason in nature why one man should be king and lord over another.[12]

Rutherford was a Presbyterian but his formulation would have been equally acceptable to the Puritan left wing.[13] Adam appeals to much the same principle in his condemnation of Nimrod in the twelfth book and Abdiel significantly makes no attempt to challenge its logic. He replies tartly that Satan owes his existence to God and has therefore no right to challenge His decrees. Moreover he was created by the Son and has therefore no right to dispute His exaltation. Lastly, obedience to a hierarchic superior is a confirmation, not a denial of freedom. The retort strikes us as unconvincing but that is because we start off with the presumption that the devil may be right. To Milton's reader, on the contrary, he was wrong because he was the devil, and doubly damned by quoting Scripture for his purpose. Abdiel's insistence is clear, even brutally clear. You are not reasonable when you disobey God's will. You violate reason by the very fact of your dissent. When you have set yourself thus against the nature of things there remains no alternative except your subordination by force, or your ultimate expulsion from the order you have defied:

> ... to subdue
> By force, who reason for thir Law refuse,
> Right reason for thir Law, and for thir King
> *Messiah*, who by right of merit Reigns.

It is a judgment which Satan recollects in Hell. "Whom reason hath equald, force hath made supream / Above his equals."[14] But the grounds of Satan's complaint, the affectation of equality with God, the refusal to admit that the Messiah reigns by merit, these things cut him off from the laws he professes to honour. The consequence is not liberty but servitude, for liberty (and it is impossible to emphasize this too strongly) is only secured by obedience to God's command:

> Unjustly thou deprav'st it with the name
> Of *Servitude* to serve whom God ordains,
> Or Nature; God and Nature bid the same
> When he who rules is worthiest, and excells
> Them whom he governs. This is servitude
> To serve th'unwise, or him who hath rebelld
> Against his worthier, as thine now serve thee,
> Thy self not free, but to thy self enthrall'd.

Now that the assumptions no longer interest us, it is easy to underrate the skill with which Abdiel makes his indictment. To begin with, he counters Satan's appeal to the Law of Nature, with the impregnable retort that the Law of Nature cannot conflict with the Divine Law. He then goes on to

present Satan's sin as a violation of "degree", a violation
which has to issue in servitude. Given this challenge to the
nature of things, this mockery of the very ground of one's
being, the only possible consequence is defeat. Satan may
commit his rebel hordes to battle. He may delay the onslaught
of the inevitable with secret weapons and atrocious puns. But
in the end the "Chariot of Paternal Deity" which as Wilson
Knight rapturously remarks "is at once a super-tank and a
super-bomber" must move to its terrible victory over God's
enemies.[15] It is a brutal climax no doubt, but one which
helps to hammer home Raphael's warning:

> ... let it profit thee to have heard
> By terrible Example the reward
> Of disobedience; firm they might have stood,
> Yet fell; remember, and fear to transgress.

The account of the Creation follows. God is presented as
having planned it to fill up the "vacant room" caused by the
expulsion of the apostate angels (VII, 150 ff.). This kind of
motivation strikes us as absurd but, as Professor McColley
demonstrates, it was accepted without hesitation by Milton's
contemporaries.[16] The description of the Creation itself is a
compact but inclusive summary of the material embodied in
innumerable hexamerons. Milton departs from tradition in
assuming a pre-existent chaos but the assumption is obviously
essential to his narrative. He also simplifies his account by
postponing the dialogue on astronomy till the eighth book
instead of associating it, as is usual, with the first, second or
fourth day of the Creation.[17] The dialogue, which has excited
as much comment as anything else in the epic, has been
referred by McColley to a controversy between Wilkins and
Ross.[18] Wilkins was Cromwell's brother-in-law and a founder
of the Royal Society. Ross, among other things, was King
Charles's chaplain. Perhaps it is worth noticing that Raphael
sides with Ross. He is sarcastic about the Ptolemaic System,
plays non-committally with the Copernican, poses the hypothesis of a plurality of worlds and tells Adam to be lowly wise
and leave astronomy to heaven. Adam, like a good schoolboy,

repeats the lesson after him and proceeds to tell a story of his own. Raphael listens to him "heavenly meek"—a beautiful touch this of hierarchic courtesy—while Adam talks of his own and Eve's creation. It is a story which we cannot understand without a conscious effort to do so. For since we do not believe with Aquinas that "order consists in inequality", since at best we can make only a metaphor of degree, since we look on the hierarchic principle as an ornamental conceit, we are compelled to regard "Hee for God only, shee for God in him" as one more specimen of Miltonic egoism. On the contrary it typified the deepest and most impersonal feelings of the time. "Married Folkes", declares William Perkins with brutal directness, "are either Husband or Wife. The Husband is he which hath authoritie over the wife."[19] Simon Goulart goes even further: ". . . in the dignity and power of man over a woman (as in all other authority and pre-eminence) the glory of God shineth clearly."[20] Calvin asserts that "it is a great honour that God has appointed her [the woman] to the man as the partner of his life, and a helper to him, and has made her subject to him as the body is to the head".[21] Handbook after handbook on matrimony insisted with tireless unanimity that man is to woman as Christ is to the Church. It is against the background of this insistence, the insistence that the woman can only be herself in being subject to man, the insistence of St. Paul that man is "the image and glory of God" but woman "the glory of the man", it is against this reiterated conviction that Adam's narrative needs to be assessed. And when we read it thus we know that he is doomed from the outset. We know that even before he has considered eating the fruit his uxoriousness has sown the seeds of his disaster. When Adam says to God:

> Thou in thyself art perfet, and in thee
> Is no deficience found,

we recognize the admission of God's infinity. But when he says of Eve:

> . . . when I approach
> Her loveliness, so absolute she seems

And in herself compleat, so well to know
Her own, that what she wills to do or say,
Seems wisest, vertuousest, discreetest, best.

we must force ourselves to acknowledge the latent blasphemy.
Eve is not God, but a creature, and a creature, moreover,
whose happiness consists in her being subject to Adam. It is
Adam's duty to rule her as his reason rules his passions. As
Augustine puts it: "Just as in the human soul there is one
element which takes thought and dominates, another which
is subjected to obedience, so woman has been created cor-
poreally for men: for though she has indeed a nature like that
of man in her mind and rational intelligence, yet by her
bodily sex she is subjected to the sex of her husband, much as
appetite, which is the source of action, must be subjected to
reason if it is to learn the rules of right action."[22] So when
Adam ecstatically confesses:

All higher knowledge in her presence falls
Degraded, Wisdom in discourse with her
Loses, discount'nanc'd, and like Folly shewes;
Authority and Reason on her waite. . . .

we are required not to applaud but to condemn. We need to
remember with Sir Thomas Browne that the temptation of
the man by the woman may be "the seduction of the rational
and higher parts by the inferior and feminine faculties".[23]
When we do so we shall realize that, given the values Milton
accepts, there can be no more blatant example of abject and
grovelling idolatry. It is not surprising that the angel answers
"with contracted brow". The wonder is that he is as moderate
and courteous as he is. He tells Adam that true love "has its
seat in reason". This may seem paradoxical to us but it is
merely Raphael's way of insisting that the order of the
universe is ultimately rational and that love has its fulfilment
in the ultimate order of things. It leads up to heaven as the
order of the creatures leads to their creator. It is the means,
the instrument by which body can work up to spirit and man
be translated into his heavenly paradise. Love, true love,
which guides all things to their destiny is thus not the slave of

a corrupt and localized passion, but the symbol and sanctity of an enduring order:

> In loving thou dost well: in passion not
> Wherein true love consists not.

Having said this Raphael can proceed to his final admonition:

> Be strong, live happie, and love, but first of all
> Him whom to love is to obey, and keep
> His great command: take heed lest passion sway
> Thy judgment to do aught which else free Will
> Would not admit.

The warning, besides reflecting the outlines of Adam's transgression, parallels the warning provided for Eve in her dream. Milton's audience, reading these passages, would have known what would take place and exactly how it would happen. They would know that nothing had been left undone, that all necessary information and counsel had been given. And so, as Milton changed his notes to tragic, they would have read on with an obsessing fascinated interest as Adam and Eve, possessed of everything necessary to preserve their innocence, marched open-eyed and reckless to ultimate disaster.

IV

A week after Raphael's departure the second and successful temptation takes place. John Swan, who likes being precise about such things, insists that it took place on the twenty-second of April.[1] But Milton says nothing about this and since Eden is in a state of eternal spring it is impossible to tell from the state of the vegetation. However, we know that on the previous night Satan disguised as a mist had made an underground entry into Paradise.[2] Light now dawns, the "Earth's great Altar" sends up praise to the Creator[3] and Adam and Eve celebrate the occasion by indulging in the pre-lapsarian equivalent to a lover's quarrel. The dispute arises when Eve suggests a division of labour. Adam is to wind the woodbine and direct the clasping ivy while Eve does what she can in a grove of roses "intermixt with Myrtle". Adam replies cautiously that such a parting is dangerous, that Satan is awaiting an opportunity for his assault, and that the wife is safest by the side of her husband. Eve, though she replies with "sweet austere composure", obviously regards this as a slur on her integrity, so Adam has to assure her that he knows she will not succumb to temptation, but merely wishes to spare her the insult of being tempted. Eve, however, is not interested in a fugitive and cloistered virtue and insists on sallying forth to meet her adversary. [4] Adam then reluctantly lets her go but not before arming her with this advice:

> O Woman, best are all things as the will
> Of God ordained them, his creating hand
> Nothing imperfet or deficient left
> Of all that he created, much less Man,
> Or ought that might his happie state secure,
> Secure from outward force; within himself
> The danger lies, yet lies within his power:
> Against his will he can receave no harme.
> But God left free the Will, for what obeyes
> Reason, is free, and Reason he made right,
> But bid her well beware, and still erect,
> Least by some faire appeering good surpris'd
> She dictate false, and missinforme the Will
> To do what God expressly hath forbid.

The warning complements that which Raphael gives to Adam. It makes it clear that Eve sins because her faculty of reason is deceived while Adam sins by surrendering his will to his passions. The two faults taken together—a defective understanding and a disobedient will—make up the mortal sin, the compendium of every possible error. [5] As usual the antithesis is confirmed by other contrasts. The warning on each occasion is given by a hierarchic superior. The temptation on each occasion is the work of a hierarchic inferior. Presented thus these details may seem trivial but they are in fact indispensable to the pattern of transgression. As Goodman glumly remarks:

Thus at length hee [Satan] perswades the Serpent to be his Agent and factor, desiring to invert and overthrow the whole course of nature, when the basest creature shall give advice and direction to the best, in the highest point of religion; and that the Serpent should deceive the woman, the woman her husband (the feete must guide and direct the head), notwithstanding God's forewarning and threatening to the contrary.[6]

It is this direction of the higher by the lower, this systematic violation of the government of things, which dominates the action of the ninth book. Every phrase drives home the subjection of reason to appetite, the complete enslavement of the mind to the body. Milton does not hesitate to be unconventional in order to secure his effects. He goes out of his way to draw attention to Eve's gluttony.[7] He compares the fruit to an intoxicating wine, minutely describes the carnality it fosters and degrades the romantic love of Adam for Eve into irrational and destructive lust.[8] He does these things although there is no real precedent for doing them so that, when we come to his declaration that "understanding ruled not", we may be deeply and inescapably conscious of the terrible significance which lies behind the formula. So as Eve moves on towards her ordeal wrapt in a cloud of perfume and waited on possibly by a pomp of graces, we are required to watch with unrelaxing vigilance the words which record her progress to catastrophe.

First and foremost we must observe the subtlety of the Serpent's arguments. Milton here is elaborating craftily on a familiar theme of seventeenth century theologians. Andrewes, for example, devotes several pages to discussing the devil's rhetoric.[9] Downame asserts that Satan proceeds by "equivocations and sophisticall eclenches".[10] Lawson takes pains to point out that the serpent "doth not single out any of God's *moral* precepts or prohibitions. For these were too deeply implanted in the soul, and of clearer light, but he makes choyce of that positive precept which was not so obvious to reason, and seemed to have some mystery in it, and to admit some latitude for a *subtle discourse*".[11] Thus when Milton compares the serpent to an Athenian orator he is doing more than chide his classical leanings. The serpent, after all, has an important job to do. His eloquence helps him to do it better, and he is further helped by being impossibly handsome and greatly superior to anything out of Ovid. Moreover, he knows Eve well enough to play upon her vanity. He fawns on her, bowing his "sleek enamell'd Neck". He pays her a preposterous tribute—"Fairest resemblance of thy Maker faire"—which exalts her subtly above her hierarchic status. A few lines later on he elegantly varies the compliment—"Sovran of Creatures, universal Dame". It is little wonder as he gazes at Eve with his carbuncle eyes that his words win "too easy entrance" into her unwary heart. She makes no attempt to challenge his arguments and in fact uses them to justify her transgression. She errs because she is insufficiently vigilant. Despite Adam's advice her reason does not keep strictest watch and so falls "into deception unaware". Yet for all her murderous triviality she is really no more than hapless and much-failing. We sympathize with her as she puts forth her hand to the fruit. We sympathize still as the earth gives signs of woe. We remember the same earth smiling on the nuptials of Eve and Adam and the hills of heaven putting forth flowers as the wheels of the Son's chariot moved to victory.[12] We remember these things, and the memory of their beauty blinds us for the moment to the crime that we are witnessing. Then the recollection is shattered by the aftermath of Eve's sin, by her idolization of the tree, her contemplation of murder, and by the confirmation of her soul in the practice of evil. Yet despite all this she is still not alienated from us, and Adam catches some of our own feelings in the forlorn, horror-struck words with which he greets her:

> O fairest of Creation, last and best
> Of all Gods Works, Creature in whom excell'd
> Whatever can to sight or thought be formd,
> Holy, divine, good, amiable, or sweet!
> How art thou lost, how on a sudden lost,
> Defac't, deflourd, and now to Death devote?

The last line is especially poignant with its heavy, heart-

broken sequence of d's, its hint of a lost Eden in the overtones
of "deflourd" and its listless acceptance of dedication to
death. Yet touching as the words undoubtedly are, they make
it evident that Adam is doomed from the outset. Eve may be
the last of God's works, but it is Adam, not she, who is the
best. When he forgets that this is so, when he calls Eve the
"fairest of Creation", when the majesty we associate with
"holy" and "divine" is linked to the romantic pathos of
"amiable or sweet" it is plain to us that he has chosen disaster. Having said this he has to indulge in the heroics of

> ... I feel
> The Bond of Nature draw me to my owne,
> My owne in thee, for what thou art is mine;
> Our state cannot be severd, we are one,
> One Flesh; to loose thee were to loose my self.[13]

and Eve must reply in terms of the same frivolity:

> O glorious trial of exceeding love
> Illustrious evidence, example high!

I have used the word "frivolity" deliberately. It may shock
a good many of my readers, but this only proves that the
sensibilities of Milton's audience were radically different
from our own. For though we are justified in sympathizing
with Adam's predicament and though it is to Milton's credit
that he finds a human problem where others see only a theological formula, though we may applaud such self-sacrifice
as a romantic gesture, we have to condemn it as a responsible
act. We cannot approve of what Adam does and we can
approve still less the alacrity with which he does it. There is
in him no will, no power of resisting temptation. He does not
even hesitate as Eve hesitates. His idolatry, all the more
offensive because it is clear-eyed,[14] is an insult to the righteousness to which he is meant to conform. Because he sins thus,
because he surrenders his judgment to his passions, it follows
that "reason's mintage" within him must become "the
inglorious likeness of a beast". Everything that follows
assumes this degradation. Intoxication follows gluttony and
is succeeded by carnal desire. The two, far from regretting

what they have done, congratulate themselves on their good
sense in doing it. Then, as the spasm of exhilaration expires,
their eyes are opened and they find their honour stripped
away. Milton drives this home by using a well-known simile:

> So rose the *Danite* strong
> *Herculean Samson* from the Harlot-lap
> Of *Philistean Dalilah*, and wak'd
> Shorn of his strength. . . .

It is a simile which we treasure chiefly as an anticipation
of Milton's future tragedy. So we need to remember that
twenty-five years ago, in *The Reason of Church Government*,
Milton had talked of Samson as "disciplin'd from his birth
in the precepts and practice of Temperance and Sobriety,
without the strong drink of injurious and excessive desires".
Samson's eyes in that elaborate allegory were "the fair, and
farre-sighted eyes of his natural discerning" and his hair "the
golden beames of Law and Right".[15] But these associations
are by no means peculiar to Milton. Much the same thing is
said for instance by Bishop Reynolds in his discussion of the
effects of the Fall.

> We are . . . to remember, that there is in Man, by reason of
> his general *Corruption*, such a distemper wrought, as that there
> is not onely *crookednesse* in, but *dissension* also, and fighting
> betweene his parts: And, though the Light of our *Reason* be by
> Man's Fall much dimmed and decayed; yet the remainders
> thereof are so adverse to our unruly *Appetite*, as that it laboureth
> against us, as the *Philistims* against *Samson*; (or rather indeed as
> *Dalilah*, for *Samson's* eyes were truly put out before ever the
> *Philistims* were upon him) it laboureth, I say, to deprive us
> of those Reliques of Sight which we yet retaine.[16]

The simile therefore has a function to fulfil. It implies that
this newly-found knowledge of the flesh is secured and perverted by blindness to the things of the Spirit. Adam and Eve
have their eyes opened indeed, but they see no longer with
the eyes of natural innocence.

> Bad Fruit of Knowledge, if this be to know,
> Which leaves us naked thus, of Honour void,
> Of Innocence, of Faith, of Puritie . . . .

Purchas grows lyrical as he speculates on this nakedness:

> Their eyes were opened to see their nakednesse: *naked* they were
> of *divine* protection and favor, naked of *Angelicall* guard and
> custodie, naked of *Humane* puritie and holinesse, naked of
> dutifull *subjection* from the rebelling Creatures; naked in *soule*,
> naked in *Body*, naked of *Happinesse*, naked of *Hopes*, exposed
> naked to the fierce *Wrath* of that God, from whom to bee
> hidden was impossible . . . and to whom to appeare was
> intolerable.[17]

If Adam and Eve are really as naked as all this it is little
wonder that they cover themselves with banyan leaves (not
fig leaves). But in acknowledging their guilt they cannot
cleanse it. They cannot revoke the defiance of order which
they have set in motion, they cannot rewrite and they can
barely recollect the law of nature which their transgression
has defaced. Within the microcosm chaos is come again and
degree is suffocated in lawless, murderous misrule:

> They sate them down to weep, nor onely Teares
> Raind at thir Eyes, but high Winds worse within
> Began to rise, high Passions, Anger, Hate,
> Mistrust, Suspicion, Discord, and shook sore
> Thir inward State of Mind, calm Region once
> And full of Peace, now tost and turbulent:
> For Understanding rul'd not, and the Will
> Heard not her lore, both in Subjection now
> To sensual Appetite, who from beneathe
> Usurping over sovran Reason claimd
> Superior sway:[18]

Three consequences follow from this usurpation. The first
is death: the corruption of the body which proceeds from and
reflects the corruption of the mind. As Aquinas puts it:

> God bestowed this favour on man in his primitive state, that
> as long as his mind was subject to God, the lower powers of
> the soul would be subject to his rational mind, and his body
> to his soul. But inasmuch as through sin man's mind withdrew
> from subjection to God, the result was that neither were his
> lower powers wholly subject to his reason, whence there fol-
> lowed so great a rebellion of the carnal appetite against the

reason; nor was the body wholly subject to the soul; whence arose death and other bodily defects.[19]

The second consequence is the propagation of this depravity in space, the overflowing of sin upon the creatures. Goodman proclaims this with his usual gloomy relish:

> Man, who was principally ordained for God's service, as all other creatures for man; man (I say), being *nexus et naturae vinculum*, it must necessarily follow, that all the rest of the creatures, which were bound and knit together in man, should likewise be inordinate and overflow their owne banks; if the Captaine and guide first break the ranke, no marvell if the soldiers fall to confusion.[20]

Calvin is so excited by the occasion that he breaks all his own rules by indulging in a simile:

> Nor ought it to seem absurd, that, through the sin of man, punishment should overflow the earth, though innocent. For as the *primum mobile* rolls all the celestial spheres along with it, so the ruin of man drives headlong all those creatures which were formed for his sake, and had been made subject to him.[21]

But the relationship is even more clearly defined in these words of a nonentity, Daniel Dyke:

> Man is truely called a little world, and in him wee may see an image of that in the greater world. Now in man, as created of God, the affections, called the unreasonable part, as beeing common to us with bruites, were subjected to reason and so shewed how by like proportion in the great world the unreasonable creatures should be subject to the reasonable. But when once order was broken in the little world, then it was broken also in the other, and when reason lost his authority over affection, then man also lost his sovereignty, over the creatures and his slaves became rebels.[22]

The third and best known consequence of this rebellion is the transmission of evil in time, the death of posterity in the loins of Adam. To suggest how the seventeenth century felt about this I cannot do better than quote once more from Purchas:

As in the Bodie Politike the Act of the Prince is reputed the Act of the whole; the Consent of a Burgesse in Parliament bindeth the Citie which he representeth; and as in the naturall Bodie the whole Bodie is lyable to the guilt of that fact which the head or hand hath committed: as a root to his branches, a Fountaine to his streames, doth convey the goodnesse or badnesse which it selfe hath received: so stands it betwixt us and Adam our naturall Prince, the Burgesse of the World, the Head of this humane Bodie and Generation, the Root and Fountaine of our Humanitie.[23]

It is these three consequences considered jointly, this vision of enmity between all created things, this chaos in man's mind and in the cosmos, this intolerable order of events where depravity feeds and propagates depravity, it is against this background of unrelieved pessimism that the action of the last books of *Paradise Lost* is located. Milton has prepared very carefully for this climax. The hostility between reason and the passions is persistently implied before it is asserted. We are told there is hate in the minds of Eve and Adam, before we see it growing up between them. So when the earth during the transgression groans and gives "signs of woe" we expect the creatures to be drawn headlong into ruin. We may perhaps remember *Romans* viii, 22: "For we know that the whole creation groaneth and travaileth in pain together until now"—but even if we do not, we are still prepared for the omnipresent corruption which St. Paul's words suggest. When the Son descends to deliver judgment these developing discords are further reinforced. There is hostility between Adam and the earth he tills. There is enmity incipient in the "Despotic Power" which man is given in order to punish woman.[24] It is a conflict which Milton expands and complicates as Sin and Death take up the melancholy story. We find them where we expect to, at the Gates of Hell, snuffing delightedly the scent of carnage on earth. The "great altar" which that very morning had sent up praise to the Creator now sends up the "savour of Death from all things there that live". The omen persuades the two to build a causeway from "Hell gates" to the top of the world to improve communications in their prospective empire. There is a good deal of jubilant burlesque and then, when the pair meet Satan on his way homeward, some ceremonial manoeuvres by the infernal Trinity. While Satan proceeds to his humiliation in Hell, his accomplices take up the reins of misgovernment. "Plenipotent on Earth of matchless might." Sin asks Death what he thinks of his Empire and Death replies indifferently that it would be a better Empire if there were more to eat. Sin then advises him to get to work on the inferior creation while she "seasons" man as the tastiest dish of the evening. The Angels now begin to make various alterations in the cosmos so as to reflect the depravity of things. Milton is not sure exactly what happened. The sun may have been made to change its course or, on the other hand, the "Centric Globe" may have been "push'd oblique". But anyway the planets are taught to meet in "Synod unbenigne" in order to produce the Cambridge climate. As a result of these changes we now have snow, hail, gusts, vapours, mists and pestilent exhalations. Milton ornaments the account with a complicated catalogue of winds which, according to Professor Whiting, is really very simple if you look in the right atlas.[25] But even those who cannot afford an atlas can still listen to the proper names as they clash and clang in their superb and symbolic commotion. The climax of this fantastic catalogue of calamity is Adam's long and tortured self-interrogation which leads at last to an unreserved admission of his guilt:

> . . . all my evasions vain
> And reasonings, though through Mazes, lead me still
> But to my own conviction: first and last
> On mee, mee onely, as the sourse and spring
> Of all corruption, all the blame lights due;

But even this confession cannot bring Adam peace and it remains, with beautiful aptness, for Eve, who helped to destroy him, to take the first steps towards his restoration. Her approach drives Adam to one more petulant outburst. Then as the poetry quietens down into the secure, flowing rhythm of Eve's supplication it becomes evident that the crisis has been passed.[26] In this universe of immense and brooding desolation, against all the horror of the implacable and unknown, the innate chivalry of two ordinary and very frightened people is slowly but invincibly reasserted. There is all the difference in the world between the understanding which Adam here displays and his operatic gestures in the ninth book. There is no comparison possible between the pampered egoism of Eve during the Fall and the self-sacrificing majesty which she now exhibits. In this newly-found comprehension, this humanity won from the frontiers of defeat, Milton's faith in man's goodness is splendidly affirmed. It is a faith which, if anything, has grown deeper and more tolerant with the years. For in "Adam Unparadiz'd" Adam does not repent thus. He is as Milton writes "stubborn in his offence". Before he can see the error of his ways he has to be reasoned with by Justice, admonished by the Chorus and intimidated by the masque of evils which Milton postponed to the eleventh book of the epic.[27] The draft shows us a criminal driven to confession by fear. *Paradise Lost* shows us two people ennobled by adversity, acknowledging their unworthiness of their own free-will. The twenty-five years which separate the versions, those years which scarred England with the bitterness of civil war, which shattered the glass walls of innumerable Utopias, those years which brought Milton defeat and disillusion have taught him nothing except to believe in Man. It is an unusual lesson and one which ought to qualify the charge of pessimism which is levelled against the last books.

V

It is noteworthy that in two and a half centuries of Miltonic criticism the last books of *Paradise Lost* have been less and less approved. Hume thought of them highly enough when he claimed that they surpassed "all those tedious Stories and the vain-glorious boastings of *Homeric Heroes*".[1] But Addison, not long after, was more cautious: "these two last books can by no means be looked upon as unequal parts of this divine Poem."[2] Thyer admitted that the last book lacked "poetick decoration" but went on to claim that the strength and clearness with which Milton had expressed the truths of Christian theology "must excite no less admiration in the mind of an attentive reader, than the more sprightly scenes of love and innocence in Eden, or the more turbulent ones of angelick war in Heaven".[3] Johnson however did not think the last books worth mentioning. Bailey follows in his footsteps by quoting from them once and neither Pattison nor Raleigh are more generous. In our own time indifference has changed to hostility. Thus Mr. C. S. Lewis, who has done as much as anyone else to restore *Paradise Lost* to the common reader, remarks that "Such an untransmuted lump of futurity, coming in a position so momentous for the structural effect of the whole work, is inartistic. And what makes it worse is that the actual writing in this passage is curiously bad".[4] Dr. Tillyard finds himself harassed by Milton's pessimism: "In the last books pessimism has got somehow into the texture of the verse, causing a less energetic movement."[5] Sir Herbert Grierson qualifies this by arguing that "the pessimism of *Paradise Lost* is the pessimism inherent in Evangelical Christianity and the Puritan outlook on life". But he, too, like everyone else, is convinced that "the least interesting part of the poem is doubtless the visions and narrative of the last books".[6]

Now, in the face of such unanimous disapproval, it is only too easy to enter into apologies, to claim that Milton changed his mind, or lost his head, or was stricken with one of those mysterious illnesses with which we assail poets in their less likeable periods. These are excuses which I should be only too glad to make since I myself am not in love with the last books. I do not deny that they are bleak and barren, and that the discipline they preach is an insurance against sin rather than a basis for virtue. I agree that the ideal set forth is one of contempt for the world rather than charity towards it, that Milton shows us the stoic indifferent to events and not the

crusader whose righteous actions redeem them. But to judge
the last books solely by such drabness, to concentrate on the
colouring of despair, is to ignore the ground-swell of insistent
courage which struggles against and so very nearly subdues it.
When you apologize, it is usually for something which you
cannot explain. And because I think that there is something
in the last two books which is very much worth explaining I
must ask my readers to try to see them anew.

First of all it should be clear that whatever Michael's survey may amount to, he himself does not think it pessimistic.
When he takes Adam to the top of that fabulous mountain to
show him the world according to Ortelius's atlas[7] he makes
the moral of his sermon plain:

> *Adam*, thou know'st Heav'n his, and all the Earth,
> Not this Rock onely; his Omnipresence fills
> Land, Sea, and Aire, and every kinde that lives,
> Fomented by his virtual power and warmd:
> All th'Earth he gave thee to possess and rule,
> No despicable gift; surmise not then
> His presence to these narrow bounds confin'd
> Of Paradise or *Eden*: this had been
> Perhaps thy Capital Seate, from whence had spred
> All generations, and had hither come
> From all the ends of th'Earth, to celebrate
> And reverence thee thir great Progenitor.
> But this praeeminence thou hast lost, brought down
> To dwell on even ground now with thy Sons:
> Yet doubt not but in Vallie and in plaine
> God is as here, and will be found alike
> Present, and of his presence many a signe
> Still following thee, still compassing thee round
> With goodness and paternal Love, his Face
> Express, and of his steps the track Divine.
> Which that thou mayst beleeve, and be confirmd,
> Ere thou from hence depart, know I am sent
> To shew thee what shall come in future dayes
> To thee and to thy Offspring; good with bad
> Expect to hear, supernal Grace contending
> With sinfulness of Men; thereby to learn
> True patience, and to temper joy with fear

And pious sorrow, equally enur'd
By moderation either state to beare,
Prosperous or adverse:

The argument of this passage needs to be carefully considered. To begin with Michael says that God is omnipresent and that his goodness permeates the whole world as well as Eden. Then he goes on to make the startling assertion that his forthcoming pageant of world history is a *proof* of this omnipresence. A modern reader, at this stage, might well raise his eyebrows and ask how this parade of confusions, accusations, and lazar-house calamities could possibly be construed as proclaiming the power and providence of God. The key, I suggest, is in that central phrase: "supernal Grace contending / With sinfulness of Men." And the nature of this antithesis only becomes apparent when we try to recover the vision of complete and radical depravity which that one word "sinfulness" is intended to evoke. In Milton's England one did have to be a Puritan to see it. Ussher, that great liberal, maintained as vehemently as Calvin that man, after Adam's fall, was "dead in Sin as a loathsome carrion".[8] Burton and Montaigne insisted that he was worse off than any animal. Goodman becomes quite comic in his desperate anxiety to prove this:

> The little chirping birds (The Wren, and the Robin) they sing a meane; the Goldfinch, the Nightingall, they joyne in the treble; the Blacke bird, the Thrush, they bear the tenour; while the foure footed beasts with their bleating and bellowing they sing a bass. . . . Only man, as being a wild and fierce creature, hath no certaine note or tune . . . his instruments are the guts of dead creatures, a token of his crueltie, and the remainder of his riot.[9]

The Reverend John Moore, as he contemplates this riotousness is plainly red with furious indignation:

> . . . This corruption of our flesh (so long as we live) sendeth out the filthy scum of all uncleannesse, which continually broyleth and wallopeth in our nature, foaming out such filthy froath and stinking savour to our mindes, that it is not onely

F   81

detestable to the soule of the regenerate, but also abasheth the very naturall man to looke into such a loathsome stye of sin and sincke-hole of iniquities.[10]

But even such bitterness pales before Purchas's invective as he gloomily contemplates "Man's degradation; the order of his inordinate Retrograde considered in threescore several successive descents and degrees of Degeneration".[11] The resonant chapter-heading gives only a faint idea of Purchas's sumptuous despondency as he descends the Scale of Nature into Chaos, demonstrating at each stage with sombre relish, that man is worse than the species he is describing. His conclusion is put for him by a kindred spirit, J. S.: "Man is a Map of all the Regions of vanitie, an *Index* of all the Volumes of vanitie, a *Compendium* of all the Commentaries of vanitie."[12] Now much of this is plainly a literary affectation, but there is a fluency about the best work of Purchas and Goodman which is too persistent to be easily dismissed. Eloquence like this cannot be generated *ex nihilo*, and my feeling that it has to correspond to fundamental, and even obsessing, interests, is supported by the fact that Hakewill, who writes as a professional optimist, is among the dullest prose writers in Jacobean England.

Thus when Milton talks of man's sinfulness, I think he is assuming some such background of assent. When we grant this the trend of the last books becomes clearer. Every special dispensation of God towards the righteous is a proof of His searching and comprehensive providence. Every punishment of the wicked demonstrates His justice. Every lapse of man from his original rectitude is evidence of that sinfulness which His mercy redeems. It is a clear-cut though elementary morality and though it may not convince you, I ask you to believe that it was convincing in mid-seventeenth century England. Otherwise Michael's prologue would be merely window dressing and the *felix culpa* just a ranting irrelevance. There would be no purpose in stressing either Noah's righteousness, or Nimrod's tyranny. Milton's treatment of Enoch's translation into Heaven would be merely a capricious innovation, a pedant's assertion of his special reading. On the other hand, once the opposition I am urging is accepted, these facts begin to fall into order. Enoch is meant to be contrasted with the Giants, Noah with their progeny, and Moses the Lawgiver with Nimrod who abolished "Concord and Law of Nature from the Earth". So anxious is Milton to preserve this symmetry that he is prepared to be unconventional in his account of Enoch and to base his description of Nimrod on received tradition rather than the Bible.[13] The three prefatory visions have also a poetic function. That of Cain and Abel shows us death, the lazar-house scene the various forms of sickness "inductive mainly to the sin of Eve", and the Sons of God the types of licentiousness proceeding from the "effeminate slackness" of Adam. These scenes are intended to stress the innate sinfulness of man's nature while the succeeding ones show how the providence of God confirms and protects each movement, however sinful, of that nature to the good. Hence, when the last book begins, we are supposed to be convinced both of man's vileness and of the power of God to redeem it. Accordingly, the chaos of the state of nature is superseded by the rule of Law, and when the imperfections of government by precept have been made clear, it in its turn gives way to Gospel freedom. The upward movement terminates appropriately in the *felix culpa* and in the promise of a new Heaven and Earth.

I hope this is a reasonably fair account of the plan of the last two books. It is not a plan which of itself is pessimistic, though Milton's agony contrives to make it so. He says many things which he does not have to say, and which he would have disdained to say when he wrote the "Second Defence". His account of Christ's victory is tired and dispirited. His plea for self-control has none of the ardour of the true Cromwellian, the soldier enlisted in the service of God. When he talks of patience he couples it with martyrdom. When he deplores "the general relapses of Kingdoms and States from justice and Gods true worship" he forgets the other half of his promise in *The Reason of Church Government*[14] which is to sing "the deeds and triumphs of just and pious Nations doing valiantly through faith against the enemies of Christ". These notes persist and they are unmistakable. But I shall have deceived myself if I cannot argue that they are not part and parcel of Milton's poetic design. They are intrusions in that design, forgivable, unavoidable, the clenched, spasmodic despair of the man who will one day write *Samson Agonistes*, but intrusions nevertheless which are in no way evidence of Milton's epic intention. This comes out quite clearly in Michael's appalling description of the world "under her own waight groaning" with which he ends his prophecy of history. It is a description which strikes me as an afterthought. Michael has already described that final victory of Christ over Satan which, to the theologian, gives history its significance. It is a convenient place at which to ring down the curtain and the Archangel suggests that he is going to do so by pausing dramatically "as at the world's great period". The phase is meant to recall Christ's earlier exaltation "on such day / As Heav'ns great Year brings forth"[15] and the two exaltations are supposed to draw attention to the chronological beginning and end of *Paradise Lost*. That being so, Adam's rejoinder to Michael would sound best as one of those "glorious and lofty Hymns" which celebrate "the throne and equipage of God's Almightiness".[16] Instead it develops into a craven query as to what the just will do in a world beset by enemies. Michael makes no attempt to answer this disconcerting question. He could have used the language of *Areopagitica*, the language of the true warfaring Christian,[17] of the warrior dauntlessly defending virtue "in this world of evil in the midst whereof God has placed us unavoidably". But his gloomy prophecy does nothing of the sort. He talks dejectedly of spiritual armour, wearily opposes ceremonies to conscience, and refers to wolves and hirelings in the church in words which have no hint of the white-hot anger of *Lycidas*. The whole scene *does* nothing. It repeats unnecessarily the promise of the Last Judgment. It jars against the music of the "quiet close". In short, it shows us not Michael explaining God's providence to Adam but Milton explaining his own epic to himself, attempting desperately to find peace of mind within it, trying to discover in its massive, quietening symmetry the answer to everything he has suffered and known.

I have entered into these explanations in some detail, to define the kind of criticism which *Paradise Lost* invites. When you covenant with eternity to write an epic, you are sworn to an ideal of complete impersonality. This does not exclude your finding yourself in the poem—if it is a great poem you will probably do so—but it does exclude your writing such a poem as a pretext to find or dramatize yourself. If you wish to record each caprice and spasm of your emotion, if you are caught and held by that current of frustration with which the souls of honest men are scarred, if you can find peace no-where but in public confession, then there are other forms of writing you can employ. But if these things matter to you, they matter because you are not an epic poet. For before your conflicting loyalties can emerge into epic poetry the battle to reconcile them must have been fought and won. It is only in retrospect that you can convincingly describe it. Doubting and interrogation are merely means of deployment, means to make nobler that victory of faith which is destined to subdue and eventually to include them. Milton never achieves this certainty. He is, like all men, a creature of his time. But Milton's time, unlike Shakespeare's and unlike Dante's, could set aside no man for final greatness. Least of all could it set aside an idealist and an Utopian, a man whose demands on humanity were so impossibly high that the process of history could only degrade or insult them. In the mind of such a man there will yawn for ever a widening chasm between the vision and the fact. The last books of *Paradise Lost* reveal that chasm and not even the miracle of poetry can bridge it.

Yet if the achievement falters, the intention can still be discerned. In that overhanging struggle between good and evil which dominates the pattern of the epic, the fall of Adam and Eve is used to manifest the victory of darkness. Beginning simply as the momentary carelessness of one unwary mind, it spreads across space and into history. The apparatus of Eliza-bethan symbolism, the assumptions of seventeenth century theology, the grotesque, elaborate mimicry of Sin and Death are all used to expand and complicate this catastrophe. So also the last books show us the victory of light, the singling out first of individuals then of a nation for deliverance, the movement from the imperfect to the perfect, from the letter of the Law to the spirit of the Gospel, from the tyranny of sin to Christian Liberty. The two phases oppose, yet complement each other. Thus because Milton represents Paradise as lost by an act of mind, he can argue more effectively that the true Paradise is within. Because he formulates the first sin in terms of Renaissance psychology, he can propose temperance, the sovereign remedy of Renaissance psychologists.[18] Temperance cures those whose reason is clouded by passion. It is accordingly the theme of Michael's sermon just as obedience is the theme of Raphael's. Again because sin conventionally involves the creatures, because chaos in man's mind leads to chaos in the universe, Milton can reinforce his favourite political axiom that outer servitude is the consequence of inner depravity. This assertion forms the pivot of the argument of the last two books. Milton is able to present it more effectively by switching over from vision to narrative while he changes his real subject from theology to politics. He also utilizes the traditional belief that Nimrod was the author of tyrants and that he was responsible for the Tower of Babel.[19] By claiming that Nimrod abolished "Concord and Law of Nature from the Earth" Milton gives that tyranny a contemporary reference, and by presenting Babel as a punishment for Nimrod's presumption he makes it clear that, in his opinion, God will deal summarily with Nimrod's modern counterparts. Adam then makes sure that the lesson has been learnt by pointing out how Nimrod's tyranny is incompatible with the Law of Nature:

> O execrable Son so to aspire
> Above his Brethren, to himself assuming
> Authoritie usurpt, from God not giv'n:
> He gave us onely over Beast, Fish, Fowl
> Dominion absolute; that right we hold
> By his donation; but Man over men
> He made not Lord; such title to himself
> Reserving, human left from human free.

Michael can now argue, that, perverted as such misgovernment is, it is only the consequence of the Fall and of the original corruption of the nature of things by Adam. God's providence is thus responsible both for the punishment of tyrants and the persistence of tyranny:

> Since thy original lapse, true Libertie
> Is lost, which alwayes with right Reason dwells
> Twinn'd, and from her hath no dividual being:
> Reason in man obscur'd, or not obeyd,
> Immediately inordinate desires
> And upstart Passions catch the Government
> From Reason, and to servitude reduce
> Man till then free. Therefore since hee permits
> Within himself unworthie Powers to reign
> Over free Reason, God in Judgement just
> Subjects him from without to violent Lords;
> Who oft as undeservedly enthrall
> His outward freedom: Tyrannie must be,
> Though to the Tyrant thereby no excuse.

It is a conclusion which Milton had meditated long and nobly. Eighteen years earlier, in *The Tenure of Kings and Magistrates*, he had observed that "If men within themselves would be govern'd by reason, and not generally give up thir understanding to a double tyrannie, of Custom from without, and blind affections within, they would discerne better, what it is to favour and uphold the Tyrant of a Nation. But being slaves within doors, no wonder that they strive so much to have the public State conformably govern'd to the inward vitious rule, by which they govern themselves".[20] In the *Second Defence* he had said it again: "It usually happens, by the appointment and as it were retributive justice, of the Deity, that that people which cannot govern themselves, and moderate their passions, but crouch under the slavery of their lusts, should be delivered up to the sway of those whom they abhor and be made to submit to an involuntary servitude."[21] In *Paradise Regained* he was to repeat it once more:

> What wise and valiant man would seek to free
> These thus degenerate, by themselves enslav'd,
> Or could of inward slaves make outward free? [22]

Yet these sentences have more than Milton's convictions behind them. The analogy Plato drew between government and self-government, the Medieval comparison of the body to the body politic, the elaborate Elizabethan correspondences between the soul of man and society, the theological assumption that man's sin draws the creatures to destruction, all these would have reinforced and confirmed this judgment stamping it indelibly on the seventeenth century mind.[23] And once you have been persuaded to accept it, when you have convinced yourself that your depravity controls the misgovernment of things, when you know, as everyone in Milton's England knew, that no effort of will can break down that depravity, then it follows that only the grace of God can save you. All other remedies are useless. Action can only harden into violence and the societies you set up degenerate into tyrannies. If you rely on yourself you covenant with darkness.[24] Your history becomes the history of God's justice of perpetual damnation under the letter of the law. But the history of those whom God's grace has renovated is above everything else the history of His mercy, of the slow but irresistible progress of man towards freedom. Milton states this quite clearly in the *De Doctrina Christiana*:

> The unwritten law is no other than that law of nature given originally to Adam, and of which a certain remnant, or imperfect illumination, still dwells in the heart of all mankind; which in the regenerate, under the influence of the Holy Spirit is daily tending towards a renewal of its primitive brightness.[25]

John Weems, in more elaborate language, says very much the same thing:

> Adam when hee was made to the Image of God in his first Creation, was like to the Moone in the full; Man fallen, before regeneration is like the Moone in the conjunction, altogether obscured by the Sunne, the Image of God is then defaced and blotted out in man by Sinne; the Image of God in Man restored, is like the Moon waxing and growing by degrees till shee come to her perfection.[26]

And even the pessimistic Goodman can set aside his melancholy to confirm this:

> Thus in this great world you may observe, that first there was a state of nature which was the forerunner to the Law; then followed the law which was a preparative to the Gospell; now at length succeeds the Gospell, wherein there is the fulnesse of knowledge, as much as is befitting our nature and present condition.[27]

If it is objected that the number of the regenerate is pitifully few it can be observed that no one in seventeenth century England seriously considered himself as damned. Many may have doubted their salvation, but they did so chiefly in order to dramatize it. The catastrophic manifestations of God's justice were reminders of the Red Sea into which they had not fallen. It must never be forgotten that Milton was writing for such people, people who had heard of sin but had never heard of progress, and for whom gloomy digressions on man's degeneracy were far less frightening than they are to us. If you wanted to sound optimistic to them, you had merely to maintain that the Saints were good men and were rapidly becoming better. It did not matter very much if you simultaneously maintained that the world was a bad place and was steadily becoming worse. Such threatenings merely encouraged the Puritan to don his spiritual armour and sally forth grimly to fight for Christian Liberty. So, in these circumstances, it was sufficient to say that God would punish the evil and reward the righteous, that history showed his solicitude for the virtuous, that he had led his chosen people out of Egypt and that therefore some day he would lead his Saints into Sion. This is precisely what Milton does say, and in these words of Michael to Adam he says it with something of the old Miltonic ardour:

> Doubt not but that sin
> Will reign among them, as of thee begot;
> And therefore was Law given them to evince
> Thir natural pravitie, by stirring up
> Sin against Law to fight; that when they see

Law can discover sin, but not remove,
Save by those shadowie expiations weak,
The bloud of Bulls and Goats, they may conclude
Some bloud more precious must be paid for Man,
Just for unjust, that in such righteousness
To them by Faith imputed, thay may finde
Justification towards God, and peace
Of Conscience, which the Law by Ceremonies
Cannot appease, nor Man the moral part
Perform, and not performing cannot live.
So Law appears imperfet, and but giv'n
With purpose to resign them in full time
Up to a better Cov'nant, disciplin'd
From shadowie Types to Truth, from Flesh to Spirit,
From imposition of strict Laws, to free
Acceptance of large Grace, from servil fear
To filial, works of Law to works of Faith.
And therefore shall not *Moses*, though of God
Highly belov'd, being but the Minister
Of Law, his people into *Canaan* lead;
But *Joshua* whom the Gentiles *Jesus* call,
His Name and Office bearing, who shall quell
The adversarie Serpent, and bring back
Through the worlds wilderness long wanderd man
Safe to eternal Paradise of rest.

This is a passage which often drives me to despair. If I were to cover the next few pages with clumsy quotations from innumerable pamphlets I might suggest faintly the massive and moving finality with which Milton sums up the relationship of the Gospel to the Law.[28] Every phrase, every word almost, says more completely and more nobly what a hundred other writers have said before. Yet even those who can neither recover nor respond to this network of allusion can surely appreciate the severe yet ardent splendour of those antitheses, the upsurge of joyousness that moves in Milton's mind when he celebrates the union of discipline with freedom. No account consistent with Old Testament history could be more optimistic, more settled in its contrast of the spirit to the letter, or more assured in its statement of that inward liberty on which the restoration of outer order depends. That liberty could be described in many ways. Like Parr you could found it on *Proverbs* xvi. 32: "He that is slow to anger is better than the mighty; and he that ruleth his spirit than he that taketh a city."[29] You could argue with Roger Williams that because the sword of the spirit could subdue all kingdoms, Christ one day would lead a spiritual Israel into a spiritual Canaan.[30] You could resort to the Elizabethan eloquence of Purchas: "The freedome which Christ hath purchased for us, doth yeeld Libertie not Licentiousnesse; frees not from duties, to doe what wee lust, but makes us have a lust to doe our duties; sweetly inclining the Wil, and renewing the Minde to esteeme the Service of God, and of men for his sake the greatest freedome."[31] Or you could use the more statly and settled prose of Ussher: "Our Sonship doth not free us from service, but from slavery, not from holinesse, but to holinesse; There is a free service which befits the condition of a son; God's service is perfect freedom."[32] Yet however you may choose to describe the conviction, when you set it within the frame of Milton's epic it implies irresistibly that Paradise must be recovered from within. The pattern of Milton's planning drives towards this. The presentation of sin as a usurpation of reason by the passions, the insistence on the connection between inward and outward liberty, the Protestant opposition of ceremonies to conscience, the elaborate system of correspondences which the poetry controls and reiterates, all these foster the conclusion which the last book presents. Milton cannot avoid saying what he did say and it is ungenerous to insist that he should have said something else.

Nor can it be complained that what he said is useless. To argue this would be to imply not only the superficiality of Milton's thought but also the general irrelevance of the Puritan ethic. Such conclusions are unreasonable and untrue. Self-government is still a worthwhile aspiration and an epic which can centre its immense and complex machinery on this demand will always be meaningful to the generations which read it. The weakness is not in the beliefs themselves but in the unshakeable and manifest conviction with which those beliefs should be normally sustained. Tired in spirit, Milton cannot sustain them. There is no progression of poetic fervour to support the mechanical deployment of the epic. The emphasis is on the purely negative side of self-government, on stoic resignation and indifference to events. Milton does not even argue as he did in 1659 that the "divine excellence" of Christ's spiritual kingdom is "able without worldly force to subdue all the powers and kingdoms of this world".[33] Content simply to stand and wait, he renounces reformation even with the sword of the spirit.

Yet if Milton's last words are pessimistic, I hope I have made it clear that the design of the epic is not. Protestant and Puritan it undeniably is. But, because it is these things, it is also the permanent expression of forces, immeasurable except in poetry, which wielded the minds of Milton's generation. Even as it stands, the close lacks neither tranquillity nor courage. Ten years earlier it might have had also that perfecting rapture with which the cause of Christian Liberty was so nobly argued in the *Second Defence*. If Milton's convictions could have stood firm, if the tide of history had not shaken and subdued them, he might yet have brought to its noblest consummation that spirit of seventeenth century Protestantism of which *Paradise Lost* is still the authentic though imperfect symbol.

THE PROBLEM OF SATAN

—————=∞∞∞∞ ❖ ∞∞∞∞=—————

"SATAN", wrote Sir Walter Raleigh, "unavoidably reminds us of Prometheus, and although there are essential differences, we are not made to feel them essential. His very situation as the fearless antagonist of Omnipotence makes him either a fool or a hero, and Milton is far indeed from permitting us to think him a fool."[1] Raleigh's conclusion reflects very fairly the trend of opinion in the preceding century, which, while not always insisting that Satan was a hero,[2] invariably endowed him with his share of heroic qualities. It is only recently that critics have become audible who prefer the less noble of the opposed alternatives. Charles Williams, the first of them, in a brief but thought-provoking introduction to Milton's poetry, spoke ominously of Satan's "solemn antics".[3] C. S. Lewis then took the hint up and developed it more aggressively. Satan became for him "a personified self-contradiction", a being ultimately farcical, a creature who could not be brought into contact with the real without laughter arising "just as steam *must* when water meets fire".[4] So challenging a formulation could naturally not pass unchallenged and Professor Stoll, backed by the resources of nineteenth century criticism, demanded at some length that the devil be given his due.[5] Mr. Rostrevor Hamilton, using Raleigh's antithesis for a title, insisted that the poet had his reasons of which the Puritan knew nothing, and that the Satan created by Milton's imagination was nobler and more admirable than the devil conceived by his intellect.[6] The controversy died away except for occasional salvoes in learned periodicals,[7] but the issues it raised are sufficiently important to be discussed again in somewhat different surroundings.

Now when a problem of this kind is presented to us the first thing we need to ask about is the adequacy of the vocabulary in which it is formulated. That "hero or fool?" is a leading question is not in itself regrettable. What is regrettable is that it is the sort of leading question which is bound to result in a misleading answer. Given certain ethical systems Satan is ultimately heroic and given others he is ultimately farcical. But what we are concerned with is poetry rather than ethics and Satan considered as a poetic force is different from Satan as a cosmic principle. For when that principle becomes dramatically real, when it comes alive in the radius of human experience, you cannot bring to its poetic deployment the simple emotions of mirth or admiration. Your response to it must not be unconditional. You have to see it as an element in a concerted whole, a single fact in a poetic process. Therefore to understand its nature and function you need to relate it to the pattern it fulfils and the background of belief against which it is presented.

It is when we undertake this reconsideration that critical differences of shading begin to emerge. Our response to Satan is, I imagine, one of cautious interest. We think of him either as an abstract conception or else, more immediately, as someone in whom evil is mixed with good but who is doomed to destruction by the flaw of self-love. But with Milton's contemporaries the response was predominantly one of fear. If like Calvin they thought of Satan as "an enemie that is in courage most hardie, in strength most mightie, in policies most subtle, in diligence and celeritie unweariable, with all sorts of engins plenteously furnishd, in skill of warre most readie",[8] that was only so that they could stand guard more vigilantly against their relentless opponent. If like Defoe they saw him as "a mighty, a terrible, an immortal Being; infinitely superior to man, as well in the dignity of his nature, as in the dreadful powers he retains still about him",[9] the vision served to remind them inescapably that it was only by God's grace that they could hope to overcome the enormous forces against which they were contending. When Milton's great figure is silhouetted against this background the effect must be as Addison points out "to raise and terrify our imaginations".[10] So the heroic qualities which Satan brings to his mission, the fortitude, the steadfast hate, the implacable resolution which is founded on despair are qualities not to be imitated or admired. They are defiled by the evil to which they are consecrated. If Milton dwells upon them it is because he knows that you will put them in their context, that you will see Satan's virtues as perverted by their end and darkening therefore to their inevitable eclipse, corroded and eaten out by the nemesis beyond them. The moral condemnation is never explicitly, or even poetically, denied. Touched on repeatedly in parenthesis, it is also always there as an undertone to the imagery. Words like Memphis and Alcairo may be nothing more than brilliant names to us. To Milton's contemporaries they were darkened with contempt. When Satan was described to them as a "great Sultan" the phrase would have reminded them of tyranny rather than splendour. When the fallen angels were likened to the cavalry of Egypt, a plague of locusts and a barbarian invasion, they would have given full weight to the mounting disapproval which lies behind the simile. As for the great Satanic defiances, they would have admired them for their strength and deplored them for their perversity. To quote Addison once more, Satan's sentiments "are every way answerable to his character, and suitable to a created Being of the most exalted and most depraved nature. . . . Amidst the impieties which this enraged Spirit utters . . . the author has taken care to introduce none that is not big with absurdity and incapable of shocking a religious reader".[11] The sympathy for Satan which the poetry imposes, the admiration it compels for his Promethean qualities, are meant to be controlled by this sort of moral reaction. And the same sense of proportion should cover his intellectual argument. When Satan appeals to "just right and the fixt laws of Heav'n", when he grounds his mandate on the ultimate nature of things, and when, in betraying overtones, he couples God's "tyranny" with "the excess of joy", you are not supposed to take these statements at their face value. Other politicians have made claims somewhat similar, and Satan's assertions as the champion of liberty would amuse, rather than perplex, those who were brought up to think of him as the first liar.

But to set aside the problem at this point is to leave its most interesting elements unstated. It is right to insist that Milton's Satan is not presented in a moral vacuum, that there is a background of unremitting hostility against which his poetic presence must be built up. But though the system within which he exists is never questioned, though it is seldom ignored and frequently remembered, its immediate implications are progressively subdued. We know, and even Satan knows, that the God against whom he is contending is omnipotent. But against the settled strength of his heroism, against the desperate and deliberate valour of Hell, that fact dies down to an abstract and distant necessity. When the weight of the poetry is thus thrown in on Satan's side, the effect must be to equalize in our imaginations the relative magnitude of the contending forces. We see Satan so clearly that we can hardly see anything else, and though conscious, we are not always or inescapably conscious, of the strength and authority of the forces which control him. The conflict, then, is neither Promethean or farcical. It is dramatically real in proportion as you assent to the illusion of equality which the poem communicates.

That illusion, however, is not intended to last. In our first glimpse of the solemnities of heaven, in the deliberations of the celestial council, in the love and mercy which are poured into the Son's sacrifice, the stature of the whole infernal enterprise is meant to be implicitly reduced. But Milton's verse is not equal to the occasion. His reliance on biblical phrasing undoubtedly meant far more to his contemporaries than it can ever mean to us, but even when every allowance has been made for this difference in impact, the drab legalities of Milton's celestial style are too curt and chill to be poetically successful. It is only in the speech on Mount Niphates, when the external magnificence surrounding Satan is stripped away, that we find his stature visibly reduced and his heroic grandeur battered and corroded by the endless siege of contraries within him.

> ... horror and doubt distract
> His troubl'd thoughts, and from the bottom stirr
> The Hell within him, for within him Hell
> He brings, and round about him, nor from Hell
> One step no more then from himself can fly
> By change of place.

Pinned on this torment he is driven from concession to concession. He admits that God is omnipotent and his own revolt unjustified. He wishes that he were ordained an "inferiour Angel", only to realize that if he were less exalted he would not be less evil. He curses God's love but ends by cursing himself. He thinks of submission but his pride rejects it; then, as desperation forces him to consider the idea, he finds that the breach between him and God is so great that no atonement could possibly heal it and that, in the last analysis, he has not even the power to atone. When we are brought up in this manner against Satan's inner helplessness, his sheer inability to be other than he is, the splendour of his presence starts to crumble. It is one of the functions of the Niphates speech to effect this reduction in scale for by doing so it helps to link two conceptions of Satan which might otherwise be harassingly opposed. On the one hand we have the "apostate Angel", the leader of all but unconquerable armies, the antagonist to God in the theatre of world history. On the other hand we need to have someone whose characteristic qualities are cunning and subtlety rather than heroic valour, someone sufficiently small to be met and conquered by Adam and Eve in the arena of their original righteousness. One hastens to add that the two conceptions are not contradictory and are in fact meant to be imaginatively reconciled in a true understanding of the nature of evil. Jeremy Taylor achieves the synthesis memorably in prose:

> His [God's] mercies make contemptible means instrumental to great purposes, and a small herb the remedy of the greatest diseases; he impedes the Devil's rage and infatuates his counsels, he diverts his malice, and defeats his purposes, he bindes him in the chaine of darknesse and gives him no power over the children of light; he suffers him to walk in solitary places and yet

fetters him that he cannot disturb the sleep of a childe; he hath given him mighty power and yet a young maiden that resists him shall make him flee away; he hath given him a vast knowledge and yet an ignorant man can confute him with the twelve articles of his creed, he gave him power over the winds and made him Prince of the air and yet the breath of a holy prayer can drive him as far as the utmost sea;[12]

The same contrast is realized poetically by Milton. Satan's omnipotence against the background of evil blends into his impotence in the presence of good. The transition from one state to the other probably begins with his deception of Uriel but it is felt most inescapably in that devouring inner chaos which is revealed to us in the Niphates soliloquy. When we see Satan transfixed upon the rocks of his hatred, confirmed in evil as the servant of his selfhood, able only to do as his inner logic demands, we see him, in his limitations, more clearly as our antagonist and know ourselves sufficient to stand against him. The imagery accordingly becomes more and more homilectical; it is addressed to Everyman in the familiar traditions of the pulpit, in figures whose content is plain and unmistakable and whose moral meaning is insistently asserted. Thus Satan appearing before Uriel as a stripling Cherub, may remind us of Burton's claim that the Devil sometimes "transforms himself into an angel of light, and is so cunning that he is able, if it were possible, to deceive the very elect".[13] But Milton makes sure that we will draw the necessary inference by using the occasion for a sermon on hypocrisy. Again when Satan descends from Mount Niphates, smoothing his perturbations "with outward calme" the preacher's voice informs us that he was the first "that practisd falshood under saintly shew". When the fiend leaps into Paradise Milton begins by appealing to his audience in the country:

> As when a prowling Wolfe,
> Whom hunger drives to seek new haunt for prey,
> Watching where Shepherds pen thir Flocks at eeve
> In hurdl'd Cotes amid the field secure,
> Leaps o're the fence with ease into the Fould:

But to make condemnation doubly sure this is followed by a simile for Everyman in Bread Street:

> Or as a Thief bent to unhoord the cash
> Of some rich Burgher, whose substantial dores
> Cross-barrd and bolted fast, fear no assault,
> In at the window climbs, or o're the tiles;
> So clomb this first grand Thief into God's Fould.

And the pamphleteer in Milton cannot resist the afterthought:

> So since into his Church lewd Hirelings climbe.

After about two hundred lines of the fourth book this homely didacticism begins to have its way. Satan's dimensions are reduced so effectively that we hardly notice how, in the process, his titles lose their lustre, how the "Archfiend" of the first book becomes "the Fiend" or the "arch-fellon" and how for the first time he begins to be "the Devil". It is fitting that this new being should sit like a cormorant on the tree of life, and even his malicious leering at the happiness of Eve and Adam is well in keeping with the Satan of popular sentiment. Protestants had long opposed the exaltation of the single above the married state, thinking of it, in Ames's words as "a diabolical presumption".[14] It is only a step from this, and not a large one poetically, to make the Devil jealous of wedded love. But even before this Satan has begun to posture and protest, according to the conventions of his villainy. His pity for Adam and Eve is eventually only an elaborate form of self-pity:

> Ah gentle pair, yee little think how nigh
> Your change approaches, when all these delights
> Will vanish and deliver ye to woe,
> More woe, the more your taste is now of joy;
> Happie, but for so happy ill secur'd
> Long to continue, and this high seat your Heav'n
> Ill fenc't for Heav'n to keep out such a foe
> As now is entered; yet no purpos'd foe
> To you whom I could pittie thus forlorne
> Though I unpittied: League with you I seek,
> And mutual amitie so streight, so close,

That I with you must dwell, or you with me
Henceforth; my dwelling haply may not please
Like this fair Paradise, your sense, yet such
Accept your Makers work; he gave it me,
Which I as freely give; Hell shall unfould
To entertain you two, her widest Gates
And send forth all her Kings; there will be room,
Not like these narrow limits, to receive
Your numerous offspring; if no better place,
Thank him who puts me loath to this revenge
On you who wrong me not for him who wrongd.

No more impressive evidence of Satan's degeneration could be cited. The lamentations mingled with the macabre gloating, the hòrrific irony seasoned with complaint are all confessions of his inner emptiness. And this vacancy is reflected in the texture of the verse. Lines like "That I with you must dwell, or you with me" are symptomatically lacking in any sense of direction. Their tiredness stands in unmistakable contrast to the rock-like assurance of the Archangel's words in Hell:

Fall'n Cherube, to be weak is miserable
Doing or Suffering: but of this be sure,
To do ought good never will be our task,
But ever to do ill our sole delight,
As being the contrary to his high will
Whom we resist. If then his Providence
Out of our evil seek to bring forth good,
Our labour must be to pervert that end,
And out of good still to find means of evil;

Even the invocation here is meaningful and moving. It has about it the strength of native courtesy, the condescension of intrinsic merit, the responsibility mingled with protective guidance which, in a great leader, is noblest in defeat. How different it all is from the crocodile condolences of the Devil inspecting Paradise. And how different are the threatenings of the passage in Book IV, the palpable attempt to make your flesh creep, from the strange force of poetic concentration which settles implacably on that one word *pervert*. The words in the first book are steadfast and impregnable with the long stressed monosyllables aiding and buttressing their massive resolution. They preach perversion without apology or comment, and for the moment you feel that perversion absolute, unalterable as a fact in nature, an element in the geography of Hell. By contrast, the passage from the fourth book is forced and undecided. The level monosyllables are listless rather than militant. The being who speaks these words, torn and transfixed by self-interrogation, is one who invites this scornful comment of Zephon:

> Think not, revolted Spirit, thy shape the same,
> Or undiminisht brightness, to be known
> As when thou stoodst in Heav'n upright and pure;
> That Glorie then, when thou no more wast good
> Departed from thee, and thou resembl'st now
> Thy sin and place of doom obscure and foule.

And Satan himself is forced to accept this verdict

> . . . abasht the Devil stood
> And felt how awful goodness is, and saw
> Vertue in her shape how lovly, saw, and pin'd
> His loss; but chiefly to find here observd
> His lustre visibly impar'd; yet seemed
> Undaunted.

The form of the ruined Archangel is inexorably losing its brightness. Once indeed, under the lash of Gabriel's comments it flares into a reminiscence of its former splendour. But the "allarm'd" Satan dilated "like *Teneriff* or *Atlas*" is never quite as impressive as the "Unterrifi'd" Satan who challenges Death at the outset of his journey through Chaos. He is too concerned with winning verbal victories, with shifty deceits and elaborate evasions. He accepts (as one cannot imagine the earlier Satan accepting) the symbolic verdict of the scales suspended in Heaven. The implication plainly is that the heroic in Satan is yielding to the perverted, and that the passions which led him to war with his creator are beginning to recoil on the intelligence which released them.

In the fifth book we revert to a Satan who, chronologically, ought to be at his noblest. Instead, we find only a professional politician, a propagandist who, like all propagandists, is an ardent champion of the Rights of Man and is therefore able to be generously indignant about the despotic tendencies of government in Heaven. It is a Satan notably different from the Archangel of the first books, and those who feel this discrepancy are compelled either to assume that Milton changed his mind about Satan as he drew him, or else find ways of making the difference acceptable. One way of dealing with the evidence is to assume that Satan is chiefly what the occasion makes him. What he is, depends on what he does. The intruder in Eden is not quite the explorer of Chaos and both of them differ from the "false Archangel" whom Abdiel conquers in "debate of truth". The battle in Heaven is, we should remember, part of a Sermon preached to Adam; it is intended to warn him against an opponent who may conquer him by force of persuasion but cannot conquer him by force of arms. So the qualities stressed are Satan's specious plausibility in argument and, side by side with this, his very real ineptness when he is faced with the weapons of reason and the right. I have dealt in an earlier chapter with Satan's complaints and suggested that Milton's contemporaries could hardly have taken them seriously. But even if they were inclined to do so they would have been set right by the evidence of the Niphates soliloquy, with its betraying confession that God's service was never onerous, and that ambition, not altruism, drove Satan to revolt. The other half of Milton's poetic intention is to suggest Satan's tawdriness and triviality when he is measured against the values of Heaven. It is a tawdriness first felt in the Devil's encounter with Gabriel but confirmed now by a style which can be fantastically complicated, by speeches which bristle with the equipment of the orator, with jaunty sarcasm and irrelevant puns.

> That we were formd then saist thou? and the work
> Of secondarie hands, by task transferd
> From Father to his Son? Strange point and new!
> Doctrin which we would know whence learnt: who saw
> When this creation was? rememberst thou

Thy making, while the Maker gave thee being?
We know no time when we were not as now;
Know none before us, self-begot, self-rais'd
By our own quick'ning power, when fatal course
Had circl'd his full Orbe, the birth mature
Of this our native Heav'n, Ethereal Sons.
Our puissance is our own, our own right hand
Shall teach us highest deeds, by proof to try
Who is our equal: then thou shall behold
Whether by supplication we intend
Address, and to begirt th'Almighty Throne,
Beseeching or besieging.

The spectacle of the arch-heretic accusing the saints of
heresy (Milton frequently calls the loyal angels saints)[15] is one
which would certainly have encouraged the violent dislike
which every saint felt for Satan. And their feelings would not
have been moderated by Satan's extraordinary arguments,
his perverse insolence in calling Abdiel seditious, and his
uncouth explanations of how he was "self-begot". Such
behaviour for them would have justified Abdiel's verdict:
"Thyself not free but to thyself enthrall'd." In Satan's utter
incomprehension of the joyous obedience which binds man to
right reason, in his persistent confusion of servitude with
service, they would have seen the flaws in the rhetoric Abdiel
mastered, and the diabolic persuasions which they too must
subdue, within themselves, on the field of Christian warfare.

When we next see Satan his fortunes have sunk much
lower. He has had to journey in darkness seven times round
the earth to avoid the vigilance of the angels guarding Paradise. Now, having entered the garden by an underground
river at midnight, he pours his "bursting passion" into
"plaints" that invite comparison with his earlier soliloquy.
This time he addresses the earth instead of the sun and, just
as the sun once reminded him of the glory he had lost, the
earth now suggests to him the glory he is to recover. It is a
glory which at most can be only a shadow of his former
brightness, but Satan is now so much the victim of his eloquence that he convinces himself that Earth is superior to

Heaven.[16] The creature who finds ease "onely in destroying" is the embodiment of the evil he accepted as his good. Unable to alleviate his misery he finds solace only in making others as miserable as he is. His mind is diseased with the obsession of revenge. He talks of man as the "Favorite of Heav'n" and of the creation as an act of spite. He envies, only less than God, the "gentle pair" whom he once said he could pity. If he is good it is because he is "stupidly good" in a momentary, bewildered abstraction from himself. Yet even in this depth of degradation he can still rise to what the occasion makes him. The classics come, as so often, to his rescue, the proper names glitter to suit his serpentine stratagems and, mounting on the pedestal of an occasional simile, he becomes as lovely as temptation is to the tempted. Admittedly when the deed has been done, he slinks away to escape the judgment of God but, despite the implications of this incident, he is allowed to masquerade as an "Angel bright" and to strut through Chaos with his diabolic progeny. Meeting the infernal council in surroundings suitably Turkish, he can still outshine the stars in "permissive glory". He addresses them on the great enterprise and on his own heroism in making the adventure successful. He alludes (quite falsely) to the fierce opposition which he encountered from Night and from Chaos. He claims with catastrophic foolishness to have purchased a Universe with a bruise and an apple, and having held God up as an object for laughter he is greeted appropriately with a "universal hiss". The punishment which descends is terrible but justified. As we leave the humiliated powers of Hell, tormented by the fruits of their imagined victory, the contrast makes more reassuring the repentance of Adam and Eve and their reconciliation to the good which Satan denies.

During these last few paragraphs I have tried to suggest that what Satan is depends on his circumstances, and how his behaviour and implied stature are determined by his functions. I hope I have not suggested that he is nothing more than a collection of abstract properties, properties which can be irresponsibly shuffled to meet the demands of varying situations. But, if he is more than this, he is also more than a theological exercise, or a means of illustrating a preconceived theory of evil. He is, in short, a poetic representation, and Milton's special problem is to take those qualities which the general imagination associates with Satan and work them into a stable poetic whole. Those qualities are by no means interdependent and in juxtaposition may often seem contradictory. They can be brought together in poetry, or poetic prose, in the emotions kindled by antithesis and paradox. But, in the more spacious economy of a narrative poem, such lyrical insights are neither proper nor possible. The truth must be revealed in action, not reflection, and so the qualities which the poem portrays are most convincing when they are made to emerge from the situations in which they are presented. If Satan is heroic, he should be heroic in Hell. If he is melodramatic, he is best so in the serene peace of Eden. If he combines weakness in understanding with subtlety in debate, that combination is best revealed in circumstances which Milton's contemporaries would associate with Christian warfare. The qualities, then, are harmonized by their relationship to a fable which is constructed to imply them. They can be brought together still more closely by the disposition of that fable, that is by the divergence between the chronological and the reading order. Chronologically Satan's deterioration is neither continual nor consistent: before his fall from Heaven he is far less impressive than he is immediately after it. But the difference (made unavoidable by Satan's function in Heaven) is one submerged in the unity which the reading order stipulates, the inexorable law of Satan's degeneration which is exercised so evenly from the first books to the last.

Satan's history therefore is meant to be read poetically. You may bring to it (and indeed it is essential that you should bring to it) the preconceptions of an established moral outlook. But such preconceptions are no more than an equipment, an accepted means of reacting to the poem. They are what Milton assumes rather than what he demonstrates. Given the organization of sensibility they imply, the function of the poem is to play upon it, to use it as far as possible as a

PARADISE LOST

medium through which its own character is created and
known. To vary the metaphor a little, the poem imposes its
perspective on your feelings. The great figure of Satan and its
inexorable decline confirms and yet insensibly rearranges the
mass of beliefs and sentiments which you bring to it. You see
it as a sermon on the weakness of evil and you learn more
clearly than you can from any philosophy that evil must die
by the logic of its being. But it is also a sermon on the strength
of evil; because you see Satan created as he is, huge in the
magnificence with which the first books surround him, you
are compelled to know him as the Prince of Darkness and to
admit his dominion over the forces of history. When two facts
so apparently opposed are reconciled in one figure a poetic
synthesis has been effected. Add to that synthesis the emotions which it orders, fear of the marauder and contempt for
the liar, with wary admiration of the orator's resources, add
to these the dramatic insights of soliloquy, and the result must
make Satan symbolically alive within the universe which
Milton's epic operates. In defining or interpreting this life,
"hero" and "fool" are inadequate alternatives. They are
descriptions, not so much of the poetry, as of the moral
system which the poetry is said to recommend, or else of the
intellectual convictions which Milton's imagination is taken
to deny.

In opposition I have tried to maintain that Milton's heart
was not at war with his head and that his Satan is on the
whole what he intended to make him. Here and there Milton's
execution may falter. But if we look at his picture through
seventeenth century eyes, if we try not to impose upon it the
deceptions of our own historic and personal perspectives, its
implications should be plain and unmistakable. The failure
lies not in the depiction of Satan but in that of the heavenly
values which should subdue him. Those values are only im-
perfectly realized. So, though one half of the picture may be
painted convincingly, the other half is sketched rather than
painted. Milton's God is what his Satan never is, a collection
of abstract properties, or, in his greatest moments, a treatise
on free-will. The Son moves us more deeply, particularly in

106

the quiet, firm monosyllables in which he announces his sacrifice. But the spare precision of the language Milton gives him is lit only seldom by the ardour which should inform it. Clothed in the language of Ezekiel's vision his triumph over Satan must have its moments of majesty, but it remains a moral rather than a poetic victory.

It is I think the barrenness of this victory which makes some misunderstanding of Satan's function inevitable. His regression faces us with a sort of vacuum and though the values which triumph over him are everywhere announced they are never brought to the foreground of our assent. Milton can describe pride, and in doing so condemn it; but love is to him never much more than loyalty, and humility teaches him only to "stand and wait". He may justify God's ways but he does not celebrate them. His sense of responsibility is too contractual, too persistently concerned with the mechanics of crime and punishment, for goodness or mercy to come into being within it. Because such goodness is so seldom real within the limits of Milton's poetry it becomes possible to claim that the poet was interested predominantly in evil, or even that evil was unconsciously his good. Such conclusions are to my mind untenable. Milton knows his Satan well enough to reject him and to make that rejection a poetic fact. If that dismissal is never stabilized in its transformation by a higher poetic acceptance, the failure should not blind us to the poverty of the values Milton condemns or to the reality and force of his depiction of evil.

THE STYLE OF "PARADISE LOST"

=∞∞∞ ◇ ∞∞∞=

"THE measure", says Milton of *Paradise Lost*, "is *English* Heroic Verse without Rime, as that of *Homer* in *Greek* and of *Virgil* in *Latin*; Rime being no necessary Adjunct or true Ornament of Poem or good Verse, in longer Works especially, but the Invention of a barbarous Age, to set off wretched matter and lame Meeter; grac̆t indeed since by the use of some famous modern Poets, carried away by Custom, but much to their own vexation, hindrance, and constraint to express many things otherwise, and for the most part worse than else they would have exprest them." These are words so often read that they are seldom remembered and the result is that some adults have forgotten what every schoolboy is supposed to know. Yet the tone of the passage, its defensive harshness, and its use of adjectives like "wretched", "barbarous" and "lame" should be evidence that Milton is vexed with his problem. And a few lines later the impression is confirmed. "This neglect then of Rime", Milton continues, "so little is to be taken for a defect, though it may seem so perhaps to vulgar Readers, that it rather is to be esteem'd an example set, the first in *English*, of ancient liberty recovered to Heroic Poem from the troublesom and modern bondage of Rimeing." To those who have read Milton's pamphlets the clang of that sentence is unmistakable. The contrast between ancient liberty and modern bondage, the buttressing of the antithesis by the appeal to classical precedent, is evidence that the man who stood for free speech is determined to stand for free verse and is convinced, though unconsciously, that he is equally adventurous in doing so.

Now this is a radical assertion for even Milton to make. Yet as we thumb the pages of English poetry before him we find to our surprise that he was justified in making it. *Paradise Lost is* the first English Heroic poem to be written in blank verse. In fact, if we set aside Gascoigne's *Steel Glas* and parts of Surrey's translation of the *Aeneid*, it is almost the first poem *of any kind* to be written in that medium. Thus Professor R. D. Havens, in a survey which is presumably as exhaustive as his scholarship can make it, has found only nine poems composed in blank verse between 1605 and 1700. By contrast, in the following half century when Milton's influence was beginning to be felt, that number had risen to over three hundred and fifty and in the next fifty years even that output was doubled.[1] Figures such as these should make it clear that Milton's claims were far more than prefatory heroics. He was certainly right in stressing the magnitude of his innovation, though he may have been wrong in estimating its value or the extent of the freedom he thought he was restoring to poetry.

Our next step therefore is to describe the innovation. Having established that Milton did something very unusual we need to inquire precisely how he did it. Hitherto the account of this process has been simple and unchallenged. Milton, we assume, took over blank verse as developed in the drama, mechanized it,[2] reduced the number of monosyllables and substituted feet, reduced more drastically the number of feminine endings[3] and secured his characteristic effects by mounting his rhythmical emphases upon the grammatical emphases of his paragraph.[4] To this description one could add latinisms, inversions, periphrases, appositional clauses and the other paraphernalia beloved of Miltonic editors.[5] Opinions differ, of course, regarding the merits of this performance. Those who value blank verse for its concentration and complexity regret, not unnaturally, that Milton's style deprives it of these qualities. On the other hand those who value epic verse for its ceremonial aloofness maintain just as firmly that these sacrifices were worth while. Sometimes, like Mr. C. S. Lewis, they illustrate this contention by going back to oral and ritualistic origins, but this exploration of the history of the epic is made solely to define its qualities and function. But whether or not one doubts the value of Milton's reformation of blank verse, nobody doubts that it was blank verse which he reformed. The unquestioned assumptions are that the tradition he inherited was that of the drama, that he modified that tradition to suit his epic purposes, and that in so doing he evolved certain practices which are deplorable or likeable according to the values one accepts.

I have put these assumptions as simply as I can and should now like to suggest that they are probably untrue and certainly uncritical. For what they seem to imply is that Milton began to write his epic in blank verse by examining and modifying the available specimens of blank verse. On the contrary, I think it far more likely that he began by examining and modifying the available specimens of epic. It seems to me more reasonable to assume that his primary interest was in the genre and not the décor, that he read great epics to assess their ultimate qualities and that he chose blank verse rather than rhyme as the best possible means of communicating these qualities to the reader. Accordingly the poetry he devised for this purpose was stiff, "homogeneous" and archi-tectural, in keeping with the insight it was endeavouring to assert. It does not resemble dramatic blank verse greatly and, when one remembers it was written in the same medium, it is difficult to see how it could resemble it less. In short it is a different instrument used for an entirely different purpose. It is not dramatic verse mutilated by extrinsic epic qualities but heroic verse freed from the troublesome bondage of rhyming and thereby set free to realise its nature.

This distinction may seem subtle and immaterial. But it is important to admit it for what it implies and to realize that when Milton restored heroic verse to its "ancient liberty" he did so in order to make it more heroic. Unfortunately (and it is ironical that the achievement should be unfortunate) he also succeeded in making it more dramatic. This makes it possible to begin irrelevant comparisons, to insist that Milton destroyed whatever Shakespeare had built up and thereby to cast him as the villain-in-chief in this fashionable account of English literary history. Nobody makes such mistakes with Daniel, Sylvester and Drayton. Their verse could be nothing but heroic (it is usually not even that) and consequently it is never condemned for not being something which it ought not to be. Milton, on the contrary, writes not wisely but too well. The variety controlled by the steady persistent momentum of his paragraph, the nuances of sound and the refinements of tempo, above all that sense of fidelity to an immediate experience which occasionally springs to action in a simile—these things are done so effortlessly and aptly that we naturally regret that they are not done more often. Yet it is only accidentally that they are done at all. Though we may know nothing lovelier than the low limping spondees which tell of Ceres searching for Proserpine, though we may never forget the spangle of consonants when Mulciber falls through "dewy Eve" on Lemnos, though there is no more magnificent piece of pictorial evocation than Satan unmoved "Like *Teneriff* or *Atlas*", it is not by these effects only that *Paradise Lost* is justified. Behind the triumphs of detail is the ultimate triumph of style. And the essence of that style is that it cannot be dramatic. It involves no struggle, no movement toward conversion, no transfiguration through experience of the mind, to the recognition and acceptance of a new order of reality. It can show you nothing that you have not seen. It can tell you only of what you have always believed. Reared then upon facts which it knows to be unchallengeable, it has to reflect in some measure the uncompromising certainties upon which it is founded and to imply through its level methodical persistence the nature of these ultimate and inexorable forces which the Providence of God deploys in history.

The style of *Paradise Lost* then, is anything but dramatic and one cannot demand from it the qualities which one often demands of poetic drama. The language is not a mode of experiencing which is eventually inseparable from the complex it helps to define. It is on the contrary a method of illustration and helps to present more effectively a series of events which are independent of the poet's use of language. The poem is written in blank verse not because what it says cannot be said in prose but because it can be said more aptly and memorably in poetry. The style therefore has the virtues which such requirements stipulate: clarity, force, an unmistakable main line of assertion, and above all the sort of simplicity which proceeds from the prior assent of the reader to the precepts the poetry is expounding. And since these precepts are as general as precepts can be, the poetry which expounds them should be correspondingly general. It must never descend to the limiting concrete example. Its purpose is not to define the emotions which lie behind beliefs but to locate them and shape them in an impersonal ritual and so encourage you to know more intensely and more surely the spiritual realities which you have always known.

So it seems to me misleading to expect from such poetry either complexity, or particularity, or an exhaustive utilization of the possibilities of language. There are compensating qualities but are best defined by a close inspection of the poetic texture. And since in poetry as homogeneous as Milton's an analysis of any "representative" passage is more than usually typical of the whole, I propose to consider such a passage in detail:

> Him the Almighty Power
> Hurld headlong flaming from th'Ethereal Skie
> With hideous ruine and combustion down
> To bottomless perdition, there to dwell
> In Adamantine Chains and penal Fire
> Who durst defie th'Omnipotent to Arms.
> Nine times the Space that measures Day and Night
> To mortal men, he with his horrid crew
> Lay vanquisht, rowling in the fiery Gulfe
> Confounded though immortal.

Now the first thing to notice about this passage is its preponderance of stock epithets. "Hideous" does not limit the suggestions of "ruine" and "penal" does little to control our reaction to "Fire". Perdition has always been "bottomless" and chains in poetry are usually "Adamantine". The associations of these words moreover are not developed but accumulated. "Fire", "combustion", "flaming" and in this context "perdition" all suggest much the same thing and a similar grouping can be made of "Ethereal", "down", "bottomless", and "headlong". The next thing one notices is that there is a massing of sounds to accompany and reinforce these massed suggestions. Thus *m* and *n* occur thirteen times in the first four lines and on all but two of these occasions they occur in conjunction with an *i* or an *o*. Such combinations backed by the predominant current of meaning convey irresistibly the terror of Satan's downfall. The next line is equally successful. The slowing down of the pace and the long groaning succession of linked *a*'s are wholly in keeping with the suggestions of "chains" and "penal". This amount of inspection should be sufficient to indicate the quality of the passage. Its organization is simple and limited (in contrast to dramatic blank verse which is complex and exhaustive) but simple as it is, it is evidently unified. And since the "meaning" is so unmistakable that you cannot go wrong about it you are set free to concentrate on the things that matter, the sweep of the style, its accumulated solidity and its stately procession to an inevitable end.

The criteria developed in the preceding paragraph can perhaps be defined more adequately by considering another passage from *Paradise Lost*. It occurs a few lines after the one I have already quoted:

> O Prince, O Chief of many Throned Powers
> That led th'imbattelld Seraphim to Warr
> Under thy conduct, and in dreadful deeds
> Fearless, endanger'd Heav'ns perpetual King;
> And put to proof his high Supremacy,
> Whether upheld by strength, or Chance, or Fate,
> Too well I see and rue the dire event,
> That with sad overthrow and foul defeat
> Hath lost us Heav'n, and all this mighty Host
> In horrible destruction laid thus low. . . .

Here the trends I have discussed are easily recognizable. There are duplicated suggestions in "Prince", "Chief", and "Throned", in "Imbattelld" and "Warr", in "dreadful", "fearless", and "endangered", and less obviously in "Heav'ns", "King", "high", and "Supremacy". In fact in the seventh and eighth lines the diction becomes so conventional that the epithets are almost interchangeable. It would make no difference to the meaning if we had "sad event", "foul overthrow", and "dire defeat", or "foul event", "dire overthrow" and "sad defeat", or any of the other possible combinations. But the decisive criterion is again one of sound as well as of meaning or, more accurately, the construction of a system of sound which co-operates with and reinforces the general trend of suggestion. For this reason the sequence is chosen for maximum smoothness and the darker consonants held carefully in reserve. When they are released finally in "horrible destruction" the effect is to make more impressive and inescapable the stock evocations of "laid" and "low". This subtle management of sound prevails far more insistently than one thinks in *Paradise Lost*. But it is perhaps nowhere more successful than in this passage from the seventh book:

> The Heav'ns and all the Constellations rung,
> The Planets in thir station listn'ing stood
> While the bright Pomp ascended jubilant.

Of this quotation Raleigh remarks: "In the last line the first four words marshal the great procession in solid array; the last two lift it high into the empyrean. Let anyone attempt to get the same upward effect with a stress, however light, laid on the last syllable of the line, or with words of fewer than three syllables apiece, and he will have to confess that, however abstruse the rules of its working may be, there is virtue in metrical cunning."[6] It is admirably said, but the danger lies in the suggestion that the craftsmanship these three lines embody can be reduced ultimately to a matter of "metrical cunning". The stress management and the sound are important enough but they are only ingredients in the total effect. In this effect the key-word is probably "station". By rhyming with "Constellations" it draws attention to the contrast between "rung" and "list'ning". At the same time its assonance with "stood" stresses the connotations which both words have in common. We see that the created universe, standing still to honour its creator, echoes as it does so with the praise of his followers. The next four words as Raleigh points out "marshal the great procession". But their stateliness (weighted by the juxtaposed accents) is grounded on the immobility of "stood". Finally the last four words are all suggestive of light. This trend, strengthened by the double stress on "bright pomp" promotes a cross-reference to "Heav'ns", "Constellations", and "Planets". The effect is thus one in which sound and stress management co-operate with other elements to define and qualify the whole to which they contribute. To discuss these elements in isolation, to talk of the poem's prosody or, as is more fashionable, its language, is an unwarranted and often misleading abstraction.

Enough should have been said by now to suggest that Milton's epic style constitutes a unity and that no element in that unity is developed excessively at the expense of the rest. It is true that the order thus composed is different from those orders which now pass as poetic. The man who has no music in his heart will naturally find that he has no room in it for Milton, just as Donne too in his time has been misunderstood by those not enamoured of meaning's press and screw. But those who are willing to listen for the music of Milton's poetry will find eventually that their response to it is controlled and even harmonized by that music. They will discover to their surprise (if they have been forewarned by Mr. Eliot) that in reading Milton for the sound they are also reading him for the sense. They will find that the long leisurely sentences, the unorthodox syntax, the ablative absolutes, and the inversions are there for a purpose and that that purpose is simplicity. The deviations from the grammatical norm are made only to create a steadier, more unremitting current of suggestion, to make more insistent that interplay of sound and evocation on which the impact and clarity of Milton's writing depends. There are of course many passages which fall away from this standard. But there are many more also which satisfy them and I think that less than justice is done to their lucidity. Consider, for instance, these words of Michael to Adam which I have already had occasion to quote in an earlier chapter:

> Since thy original lapse, true Libertie
> Is lost, which alwayes with right Reason dwells
> Twinn'd, and from her hath no dividual being:

Reason in man obscur'd, or not obeyd,
Immediately inordinate desires
And upstart Passions catch the Government
From Reason, and to servitude reduce
Man till then free.

Rewrite this in expository prose and the result would run something like this:

Since your original lapse, true liberty, which does not exist except in conjunction with right reason, has been lost. When reason in man is obscured or not obeyed, inordinate desires and upstart passions immediately seize the government of the soul from it, and reduce man, until then free, to servitude.

I think the first version is incomparably the better. The accentuation of the sense by the sound, the use of words like "dividual", "Twinn'd", and "catch", the internal assonance which binds and strengthens the paragraph, all these add to the lucidity of the best expository writing a fervour and persistence of conviction which expository prose could never hope to attain. And this is for Milton no isolated achievement. He not only attains this simplicity repeatedly but even attains it in a different dimension. The craftsmanship which makes these beliefs impressive can also be used to make emotions more appealing:

Forsake me not thus, *Adam*, witness Heav'n
What love sincere, and reverence in my heart
I beare thee, and unweeting have offended,
Unhappilie deceav'd; thy suppliant
I beg, and clasp thy knees; bereave me not
Whereon I live, thy gentle looks, thy aid,
Thy counsel in this uttermost distress,
My onely strength and stay: forlorn of thee,
Whither shall I betake me, where subsist?
While yet we live, scarse one short hour perhaps,
Between us two let there be peace, both joyning,
As joyn'd in injuries, one enmitie
Against a Foe by doom express assign'd us,
That cruel Serpent: On me exercise not
Thy hatred for this miserie befall'n,

On me already lost, mee than thy self
More miserable; both have sin'd, but thou
Against God onely, I against God and thee,
And to the place of judgment will return,
There with my cries importune Heaven, that all
The sentence from thy head remov'd may light
On me, sole cause to thee of all this woe
Mee mee onely just object of his ire.

I wish that this passage could be read again and again by those who believe that Milton could only write the grand style grandly, that his "natural port" was always "gigantick loftiness". Nothing Eve says could be said more simply and directly, yet those words, so ordinary and so humanly contrite, ring always with that secure and steadfast gravity by which the finest of Milton's writing is sustained. The order, the grace of it is undeniable; yet the cadence is one of feeling rather than logic and once again it is the sound and syntax which make this cadence possible. The repeated couplings ("love . . . and reverence", "beg and clasp", "strength and stay") together with the varying but recurrent supplication ("Forsake me not", "bereave me not", "On me exercise not") establishes very quietly the reiterative melody of the passage. Then, after the fifteenth line, these devices are discarded and over the persistent throbbing *me*'s the emotion rises gently to its climax, the measured acceptance of responsibility, so different from and yet so inevitable a consequence of the plea for protection with which the passage began.

I hope these quotations with the accompanying comments have helped to define the *timbre* of Milton's verse. The diction, the prosody, and the syntax, the subtle co-operation of the meaning and music, are all of them tokens of an underlying permanence, the sweep of the grand style towards its destiny, "the enormous onward pressure" as Mr. C. S. Lewis puts it "of the great stream on which we are embarked".[7] This characteristic momentum is nowhere better displayed than in the stately progress of Milton's more memorable similes. They are inventions peculiarly his own, owing much no doubt to classical practice, but in many ways departing remarkably from it.[8] Moreover, they are so completely unlike the similes of Shakespeare that a contrast between the two is perhaps the best method of discussing the differences between epic and dramatic poetry.

The mature Shakespearean simile is only so in name. It is felt and enacted as a metaphor. You are not intended to separate the items compared and even if, at the outset, some such separation is suggested, the work of the simile is to reduce this "distance", and to bring the elements together in a dramatic identity. When Cleopatra says:

> The stroke of death is as a lover's pinch,
> Which hurts, and is desir'd,[9]

or when Isabella says:

> Th'impression of keen whips I'd wear as rubies
> And strip myself to death, as to a bed[10]

you are not conscious (and are not meant to be conscious) of "like" and "as" as forces in the comparison. The interdependence of the elements is in no way less and is very probably greater than in this personification of the same "idea" by Romeo:

> Shall I believe
> That unsubstantial Death is amorous,
> And that the lean abhorred monster keeps
> Thee here in dark to be his paramour?[11]

In fact it is clear (and I hope these quotations suggest it) that the differences in intimacy between metaphor and simile are overwhelmed in Shakespeare's later work by the higher poetic unity which transcends them. The earlier Shakespeare can write like this:

> As in a theatre, the eyes of men,
> After a well grac'd actor leaves the stage,
> Are idly bent on him that enters next,
> Thinking his prattle to be tedious;
> Even so, or with much more contempt, men's eyes
> Did scowl on Richard: no man cried, 'God save him,'
> No joyful tongue gave him his welcome home....[12]

In this comparison (which Dryden singled out for praise)[13] the leisurely movement, the absence of interplay between the items compared, and above all the tendency of the language to expound rather than to explore the conditions it presents are immediately apparent. Shakespeare reveals these qualities also in metaphors of the same period:

> Rumour is a pipe
> Blown by surmises, jealousies, conjectures,
> And of so easy and so plain a stop
> That the blunt monster with uncounted heads
> The still-discordant wavering multitude,
> Can play upon it.[14]

But these tendencies, never prominent, are rapidly submerged in that sustained, symphonic unity of implication which Shakespeare's maturer writings achieve. The language of these later plays is seldom, if ever, illustrative. It is rather a means of apprehending experience, and so the surface likenesses, whether alleged through metaphor or simile, are invitations to pass beyond them to a deeper, more comprehensive principle of order of which they are merely the entrances and symbols.

The Shakespearean simile, then, is continually tending to the formula: A is identical with B. The Miltonic simile on the other hand is best described by the formula: A resembles B in certain respects which I shall now expound to you. The *I* in my phrases is important, though in the poetry it functions not as a person but as a directing force calling your attention to the various points of comparison in the simile. Thus when Milton writes:

> So spake the grieslie terrour, and in shape,
> So speaking and so threatning, grew tenfold
> More dreadful and deform: on th'other side
> Incenc't with indignation *Satan* stood
> Unterrifi'd, and like a Comet burn'd,
> That fires the length of *Ophiucus* huge
> In th'Artick Sky, and from his horrid hair
> Shakes Pestilence and Warr.

the resemblances you are to look for are made plain. Satan "burns" like a comet and this is stressed by "fires" and "Incenc't". He is huge like a comet and this is stressed by the tenfold dilation of the "grieslie terrour". Finally he is an omen of disaster like a comet and this is stressed by the unusual concreteness, in this context, of "hair". Pushing the comparison further one notes that Satan has his headquarters in the North and that Milton has played havoc with current astronomy to put Ophiucus "In th'Artick Sky". Again Ophiucus means "holder of serpent" and Satan is called the serpent throughout the poem. But as the last two comparisons depend on special knowledge Milton is careful not to make them essential to his dramatic effect. Ophiucus is justified because it inflates the *U* sound in "huge" and "th'Artick Sky" supplies a background by its evocation of Aurora Borealis. The simile then is magnificently sustained; but all it tells you is that Satan was very large and very angry and that devils sometimes have a great deal in common with comets. If Shakespeare had written it he would have written it in half the length and in doing so he would have forced you to reconsider the nature both of devils and of comets. Thus, in the passages on death which I have quoted, the ideas utilized are stock ideas; we meet Death the Bridegroom in Elizabethan Literature as often as Death the Skeleton.[15] But on each occasion the realization is one which is proper and specific to the dramatic situation in which it is enacted. In *Romeo and Juliet* the metaphor turns on the horror of the contrast; the lover (suggested by full-bodied words like "paramour" and "amorous") is pitted against the skeleton (suggested by words like "lean" and "unsubstantial").[16] In Isabella's tense challenge the bridegroom is directly invoked. But the skeleton rattles behind "whips" and the secondary meanings forced on to "strip" and "wear". The elements brought together may be the same as in *Romeo and Juliet*; but the clenched hysteria of the metaphor is proper to Isabella just as the rich lyricism of the earlier soliloquy corresponds to what we expect from Romeo. Cleopatra's death, on the other hand, must be well done "and fitting for a princess". So the verse moves with the appropriate regal dignity touching you, as it were, from above. It *condescends* to meet you at the level of the human. The skeleton may not be far from the bridegroom; but it is there only as an almost friendly accompaniment to "pinch", a familiarity caught with matchless and moving audacity in the "strong toil" of Cleopatra's grace. Thus on each occasion the image has its local propriety, its peculiar but inevitable method of coming alive. There is something rich and strange (but always strangely familiar) generated from the stock properties of the elements the language assembles.

Milton however does not write in this fashion. His similes are heroic, not dramatic, and so with stubborn simple mindedness he proceeds to use them heroically. In other words, he uses them to illustrate a familiar, universally accepted system of facts which is external and prior to its mode of presentation. The thing said is not changed by the way of saying it, though when Milton has said what he intends to say it is difficult to think of its being said better. In addition Milton's similes are sometimes digressive; they allow you to loiter in a backwater before being caught up again in the current of the stream. But this device, characteristically Homeric, and described by J. W. Mackail as an invention of the first importance, is used very sparingly by Milton. Moreover, when he introduces such similes, they usually serve to accentuate by contrast the superhuman grandeur of the events which they relieve. Thus, the "careful ploughman" of IV, 977 ff. (kidnapped characteristically by Bentley) isolates all the more forcibly the great figure unremoved like "*Teneriff* or *Atlas*". The simile of the angels "thick as autumnal leaves" follows an epic description of Satan's spear and shield. When the audience at the Infernal Council are compared to elves we are better convinced of the stature of "The great seraphic lords and Cherubim", huge "in thir own dimensions like themselves". This tendency to heroic aggrandizement is further strengthened by Milton's sparing use of "homely" imagery[17] and by the comparative form of many of his similes; they are continually maintaining that A is bigger, better, or more beautiful than B. But it is deepened also by reverberating allusions to the mythology and literature massed behind the epic. The accumulation of detail in the complex simile, and in the multiple simile involved with the epic catalogue, the glistening of the lances of Troy and Christendom as they fade into inconsequence beside the legions of hell, it is this persistent reinforcement of each image by its past which gives the Miltonic style its secure solidity and helps it to comprehend in a satisfying order the whole procession of events which moves beneath it. "What oft was thought but ne'er so well expressed" are perhaps the wisest nine words that can be said of *Paradise Lost*. For the phrases in Milton's epic have a history as well as a function and their history is usually part of their function. The comparison of the fallen angels to autumnal leaves is beautiful in itself. But it is all the more moving when we realize how the same simile has trembled on the pages of Virgil, Dante and Tasso.[18] We are all of us impressed (or ought to be impressed) by the memorable epic description of Satan's spear. But to see how impressive the comparison really is you need to go back to its origin in Homer's presentation of Polyphemus and trace the image in its descent through Tasso and Ariosto to Du Bartas's description of Goliath. Then, when Sylvester's couplets have done their worst, you will be ready for this dismal performance by Cowley:

> *Brass* was his *Helmet*, his *Boots* brass; and o're
> His breast a thick plate of strong *brass* he wore,
> His *Spear* the *Trunk* was of a lofty *Tree*,
> Which *Nature* meant some tall *Ships Mast* should be,
> The Huge Iron head six hundred shekels weighed
> And of *whole bodies* but *one wound* it made,
> Able *Deaths* worst command to overdo
> Destroying *Life* at once and *Carcase* too.

After this sprightly example of metaphysical wit it is a pleasure to turn to someone who knows how to use these properties heroically:

> He scarce had ceas't when the superiour Fiend
> Was moving toward the shoar; his ponderous shield

Ethereal temper, massy, large and round,
Behind him cast; the broad circumference
Hung on his shoulders like the Moon, whose Orb
Through Optic Glass the *Tuscan* Artist views .
At Ev'ning from the top of *Fesole*,
Or in *Valdarno*, to descry new Lands,
Rivers or Mountains in her spotty Globe.
His Spear, to equal which the tallest Pine
Hewn on *Norwegian* hills, to be the Mast
Of some great Ammiral, were but a wand . . .

I have quoted as much of the context as is practicable, so that the reader can see the stateliness of the background, the spacious sweep from Tuscany to Norway merging into the still greater distances which the telescope uncovers. One notes too how, in the phrase "rivers and mountains", the Italian landscape makes way for the Scandinavian, and how the gentle suggestion of height in "top of Fesole" is exaggerated by the far-off vistas seen by the "Tuscan Artist". Then in the long climbing sequence of "tallest", "hills", "mast", "great", "Ammiral", that suggestion is raised inexorably to the heights of Milton's simile. So placed, the open vowels erect a cliff-face of sound. The turn from this massiveness to the fragility of "wand" is made doubly awesome by this juxtaposition. But "wand" prepares us for "Angel forms intrans'd" just as the description of Satan's Spear is made more convincing by the description of his shield. Thus the passage has a decorum and propriety in its context which is both impressive and rewarding by itself. But I think your feeling for it is enriched if you know something of the failures which have united to make its reality, of the long tradition of effort and achievement which is reduced to some sort of ideal order within it.

In this somewhat long digression I have tried to remind the reader how securely the style of *Paradise Lost* is founded upon its European inheritance. The literature of many countries has been used to make it possible. But the fruits of Elizabethan exploration also, the fresh horizons uncovered by the telescope, the newly found wealth of Ormus and of Ind, are worked inextricably into the texture of the epic. And Milton's similes not only look backwards through allusion. They also look forward through prolepsis. When Eve is compared to Proserpine we know that she will be gathered by Satan as Proserpine was gathered by Dis. When she is compared to Ceres the implication is that she will reduce Adam from God's image to "the inglorious likeness of a beast". Again when she is compared to Pandora we are compelled to think of Pandora's triviality and of all the woes which her trivial action lets loose. Lastly when to compare "great things with small" the Causeway built by Sin and Death is likened to the bridge which Xerxes built over the Hellespont, we know that the doom awaiting the infernal pair is the same Nemesis, though in proportion greater, as the disaster which befell the Persian expedition. This anticipatory usage is characteristic of *Paradise Lost* and indeed Mr. Whaler, who knows all there is to be known about epic similes, even maintains that Milton was its inventor.[19] But whatever the origins the effect is unmistakable. These huge similes reaching both backwards and forwards, with all space and all history caught in their towering span, have about them some quality of superhuman permanence. And the style which they create is permanent also; it is a style not changed by the events which are made part of it. If we accept it and honour it, it should be because of this constancy and because nothing else but that constancy could be faithful to the steadfast, unwavering providence it enacts.

It is clear therefore that every element which can be separated for inspection from the style of *Paradise Lost* contributes to what Professor Bowra calls its "more than Latin solidity".[20] There are those who find themselves dismayed by such solidity, but the defence of Milton's method cannot be undertaken by men thus hostile to its presiding logic. When Mr. Empson searches diligently for ambiguities in *Paradise Lost*,[21] when critics as perceptive as Mr. Empson inform us that the epic is not lacking in Elizabethan richness, and when Professor Cleanth Brooks goes so far as to maintain that "perhaps it is not too whimsical to call Milton's Lucifer an example of metaphysical wit",[22] I am deeply impressed but also deeply uneasy. Such discoveries are all very well and often very exciting. But the tendency behind them is to value Milton's style for its accidents rather than its essence and to overlook the order it asserts by concentrating too exclusively on its more notable by-products.

Hence if a truer criticism of *Paradise Lost* is to evolve it needs to be freed from these prejudicing distractions. Complexity, irony and interanimation are admirable qualities to demand of poetry and it would be unjust to falter in our gratitude to the critics who have taught us to demand them. But such equipment, though useful, is unwieldy; and with *Paradise Lost* it happens to be irrelevant. It is only by feeling for the *simplicity* of Milton's style that you learn to be convinced by its underlying permanence. And when you set that conviction at the heart of your response you can better define and more charitably appreciate the innumerable and otherwise inconspicuous nuances which Milton arranges to offset its unity. But if you listen haphazardly, or worse still, if you listen for something else, these details which matter so much will be overwhelmed. The ideal is to grasp the norm so firmly that attention to it becomes semi-automatic. By doing so you become more sensitive to the subordinate effects which are mounted on this poem and at the same time your recognition of those effects is qualified by your persistent reference to the ground-swell which supports them. Once you have acquired this habit of vigilant surrender you will find almost infinite variety in the seemingly tyrannical limits of Milton's music. Listen for instance to

> Jousted in Aspra*mont* or *Mont*alban
> Dama*sco or* Maro*cco or* Trebisond

and note how the repeated sounds, balanced against the tough, jostling rhythm, seem almost to catch the glitter of sunlight on armour. Listen again to

> Eccentric, intervolv'd, yet *regular*
> *Then most, when most irregular* they seem,

and note the artful inversion of the sequence after "then most", like the steps in the dance which Milton is describing. Again in "Defac't, deflourd, and now to Death devote" the heavy alliteration helps to make inescapable the horror which Adam feels at Eve's transgression and in "So clomb this first great Thief into God's fold" the huge monosyllables "like a bell tolling into the silence of midnight"[23] rivet our attention to the doom which they predict. Such examples could be multiplied indefinitely; but it is perhaps best to close the chronicle now and to insist again that this kind of local aptness is never to be valued for its own sake. If you search *Paradise Lost* for examples of dramatic particularity and vivacious vowel music I have no doubt that you will be able to find them. But often enough you will have to acknowledge that the music is unsubtle and the drama rudimentary. Even Beliel's great speech, so ably analysed by Professor Stoll,[24] is successful less as a piece of dramatic writing than as a bloom, a colouring, laid on the epic style.

The characteristic of that style is its permanence. I am insisting on the truism somewhat aggressively because, with the exception of Mr. C. S. Lewis, most modern critics have tended to ignore it. Yet to anyone who has ever sat down to write two hundred lines of epic poetry the force of the contention will be obvious. In the beginning an epic poet can do pretty much as he pleases. He can sing, shout or swear as the inclination takes him. But once he has decided what to do he will find it extraordinarily difficult not to keep on doing it. The relation between himself and his audience, the way in which he requires his poem to be read, can never, once proposed, be radically altered. At the very most it can be laboriously inflected. Certain conventions have been devised to offset this tendency: the famous beginning in *medias res*, the consequent narrative within the narrative, the relieving simile, and the heroic council. But the majority of these conventions rely on dialogue for their effect, and dialogue in the epic is a very different thing from dialogue in the drama. You have no short speeches running into each other and manipulating by their clash and recoil the necessary shift in the kind of attention demanded. Your speeches are "set" as carefully as arias and the passages leading from one to the other are as artificial as any recitative:

> To whom thus Blank Blank with contracted brow

Or, to vary the theme a little

> Whereon with sullen leer Blank Blank replied

But however you may choose to ring the changes (and Milton to his credit rings them ceaselessly) the essential difficulty remains unaltered. The landscape is the same on both sides of the bridge. So every change in *Paradise Lost* is massive, irrevocable, like a river changing its course. It is a matter, not of sensations, but of geography, an alteration accomplished slowly through great distances whose unit of realization is the book and not the paragraph.

It is clear then that there is no device which can ultimately overcome the tendency of the epic style to be self-perpetu-ating.[25] And even if there were it would be poor strategy to use it. Poets may not be noticeably more intelligent than their fellow men; but one does not need to be unusually intelligent to realize that it is uneconomical to create something which tends to be or do something and then force it laboriously to be or do something else. Even a second-class poet should be ready to make a virtue out of necessity. The first-class poet goes further: he should have the decorum and good sense not to submit to necessities out of which he is unable to make virtues.

Sublimity is the virtue perpetuated in Milton's style. In Dante's on the other hand it is probably *bel canto*, a music which is all the more reassuring because it is won from the terrors and ignominies of Hell. So the blaze of ecstasy in which the great poem terminates is not something external to the style but the coming into being of its persistent qualities. The contrast we stipulate between heaven and hell is one submerged in this growth towards reality, so completely true to the spiritual progress it celebrates. Milton's epic unfor-tunately lacks this ultimate unity for though he may tell us that he prefers "heroic martyrdom" to "tedious havoc" he can only speak, not sing, of "the victorious agonies of Saints". His style is a triumph of the superhuman. It is magnificent and memorable in his treatment of hell. But it cannot describe heaven though it might describe Valhalla. Milton sees this and, as far as is possible within his general unity, his celestial style is different from his infernal. It is a style stripped of simile and ornament, reduced as nearly as possible to the plain truth of scripture, devoid of the resources of literature or mythology.[26] But the very magnificence against which it is pitted demands that it should be animated by some surpassing ardour, that what is lost in decoration should be recovered in rapture, that you should be able to look beyond the fire of language to the supreme and governing ecstasy which creates it. The words which Milton speaks are not kindled by this ecstasy. They may rise to a climax of personal passion as in the invocation of light which begins the third book. But these heights make all the more discouraging the arid deserts of school divinity beneath them. The writing which should be purely fire and air is impeded continually by its baser elements. It has the dullness of earth without the strength of granite. It can make nothing of the Atonement but versified theology, and when the greatest of all sacrifices is demanded in heaven it can do no more than fumble with the demand:

> Man disobeying,
> Disloyal breaks his fealtie, and sinns
> Against the high Supremacie of Heav'n,
> Affecting God-head, and so loosing all,
> To expiate his Treason hath naught left,
> But to destruction sacred and devote,
> He with his whole posteritie must dye,
> Dye hee or Justice must; unless for him
> Som other able, and as willing, pay
> The rigid satisfaction, death for death.
> Say Heav'nly Powers, where shall we find such love,
> Which of ye will be mortal to redeem
> Mans mortal crime, and just th'unjust to save,
> Dwels in all Heaven charitie so deare?

THE STYLE OF PARADISE LOST

Contrast this question with its equivalent in Hell:

> But first whom shall we send
> In search of this new world, whom shall we find
> Sufficient? Who shall tempt with wandring feet
> The dark unbottom'd infinite Abyss
> And through the palpable obscure find out
> His uncouth way, or spread his aerie flight
> Upborn with indefatigable wings
> Over the vast abrupt, ere he arrive
> The happy Ile; what strength, what art can then
> Suffice, or what evasion bear him safe
> Through the strict Senteries and Stations thick
> Of Angels watching round?

The mere juxtaposition is enough to assert the difference. Milton may prefer, and passionately prefer, his Protestant heaven to his Classical hell. He may scorn the riches of Babylon and Alcairo for the "undetermin'd" circuit of his new Jerusalem.[27] He may hammer home that contempt in every contrast, in every sentiment and doctrine which his epic proposes. But he cannot make his preferences poetically inevitable. That voice which in "Of Reformation" was preparing to celebrate God's mercies can sing only in bleak and barren measures against the tepid hymns and hallelujahs of the saints. When we interpret it thus, Blake's epigram is justified, and indeed it would be surprising if there were no truth whatever in a criticism so long and so generally accredited.

Yet when we have said that Milton's style is not heavenly we have said nearly everything that should be said against it. In the heroic desperation of hell, in the immense and dangerous anarchy of Chaos, you find it in its native element. True, in Paradise it sometimes falters: there is too much talk of angelic digestion and too assiduous an insistence on the too regular eating of vegetarian meals. But no serious critic can take these lapses seriously. It is surely more pertinent to indicate how the poetry of Eden is affected by its landscape and how the music of Pandemonium, the "sonorous metal blowing martial sounds" modulates into the gentler, more nostalgic music of Paradise. The mechanics of the style remain unchanged. But the range of literary reminiscence is altered, the leisurely similes meander rather than march, the proper names soften and become appropriately idyllic. The resultant lyricism, which could be cloying more often than it is, is saved usually by an insistent sense of proportion and by the severe yet joyous formality of its ritual. The elaborate, studied, courtesy of Adam and Eve's addresses to each other helps to stabilize this structure of ceremony which is buttressed also by the recurrent hymns. One thinks first in this connection of the stately, reiterated cadence of Eve's second address to Adam and the fervid solemnity of the hymn on wedded love. Human relationships are defined here at their maximum of dignity. But even when Milton is less free to innovate, when he is tied more inexorably to the letter of the Bible, he can still achieve on earth what he cannot achieve in heaven. The morning prayer of Adam and Eve in the fifth book is a faithful elaboration of the 148th Psalm. Yet in this spontaneous tribute of a Universe to its creator one feels a pressure of poetic homage which is found comparatively seldom in the routine choruses which terminate meetings in Heaven. The style then can be human and triumphantly superhuman; it fails, and fails distressingly, when it attempts to be divine.

In concluding, one ought to reiterate that Milton's writing has its lapses, though even those may be less serious than we think, and may be magnified because we are compelled to see them behind the debris of their eighteenth century debasements. It is perhaps more damaging to allege that the style of *Paradise Lost* is not always one with its subject, that its qualities and texture are occasionally untrue to the emotions it is intended to evoke. The balance of poetic achievement is thus disturbed and it may be that it is disturbed so gravely as to affect the overall harmony of the epic. But for those in every generation who do not find this disturbance fatal it becomes necessary to put first things first, to insist again on Milton's positive attributes, on his "plain heroic magnitude" of achievement. To suggest this perspective I cannot do better than quote from someone who was certainly no willing admirer of Milton, who disliked his prosody and detested his politics. *Paradise Lost*, says Dr. Johnson, is "a poem which, considered with respect to design, may claim the first place, and with respect to performance, the second, among the productions of the human mind". It is on a conclusion very much more than Dr. Johnson's on this side idolatry that I should like to let the eternal argument rest.

NOTES

ABBREVIATIONS

The following abbreviations are used:

E.S.	Englische Studien.
E.S.E.A.	Essays and Studies by Members of the English Association.
ELH	English Literary History.
J.E.G.P.	Journal of English and Germanic Philology.
M.L.N.	Modern Language Notes.
M.L.Q.	Modern Language Quarterly.
M.L.R.	Modern Language Review.
M.P.	Modern Philology.
N.Q.	Notes and Queries.
P.M.L.A.	Publications of the Modern Language Association.
P.Q.	Philological Quarterly.
R.E.S.	Review of English Studies.
S.P.	Studies in Philology.
T.L.S.	Times Literary Supplement.
U.T.Q.	University of Toronto Quarterly.

All references to Milton's writings, unless otherwise stated, are to the Columbia University Press edition (New York, 1931-38).

NOTES

NOTES TO "MILTONIC CRITICISM: A FOREWORD"

1. This summary is intended to deal only with the immediate background to this volume and to isolate certain tendencies for comment. Readers requiring fuller information can find it in the bibliography to the 1925 edition of D. Saurat's *Milton Man and Thinker*, in D. H. Stevens' *Reference Guide to Milton from 1800 to the Present Day* (Chicago, 1930), in H. F. Fletcher's *Contributions to a Milton Bibliography* (Urbana, Illinois, 1931), in the bibliography to J. H. Hanford's *A Milton Handbook*, and in current bibliographies.

2. E. Greenlaw, "A Better Teacher than Aquinas", *S.P.*, XIV (1917) pp. 196–217; "Spenser's Influence on *Paradise Lost*", *S.P.*, XVII (1920), pp. 320–359.

3. J. H. Hanford, "Milton and the Return to Humanism", *S.P.*, XVI (1919), pp. 126–147.

4. S. B. Liljegren, *Studies in Milton* (Lund, 1919); "Miltonic Philosophy in the Light of Recent Research", *Scandinavian Scientific Review*, II (1923), pp. 114–123; M. A. Larson, "Milton's Essential Relationship to Puritanism and Stoicism", *P.Q.*, VI (1927), pp. 201–20: L. Bredvold, "Milton and Bodin's *Heptaplomeres*", *S.P.*, XXI (1924), pp. 399–407.

5. M. A. Larson, "Milton and Servetus: a Study in the Sources of Milton's Theology", *P.M.L.A.*, XLI (1926), pp. 891–934.

6. The whole movement is fully discussed by Denis Saurat, "La Conception Nouvelle de Milton", *Revue Germanique*, XIV (1923), pp. 113–141.

7. M. A. Larson, *The Modernity of Milton* (Chicago, 1926): E. C. Baldwin, "Some Extra-Biblical Semitic Influences on Milton's Story of the Fall of Man", *J.E.G.P.*, XXVIII (1929), pp. 366–401; H. Fletcher, *Milton's Semitic Studies and Some Manifestations of Them in His Poetry* (Chicago, 1926) and *Milton's Rabbinical Readings* (Urbana, Illinois, 1931).

8. M. H. Nicholson, "The Spirit World of Milton and More", *S.P.*, XXII (1925), pp. 433–52; "Milton and Hobbes", *S.P.*, XXIII (1926), pp. 405–33; "Milton and the *Conjectura Cabbalistica*", *P.Q.*, VI (1927), pp. 1–18.

9. J. H. Hanford, "The Chronology of Milton's Private Studies", *P.M.L.A.*, XXVI (1921), pp. 251–314; "The Youth of Milton", *Studies in Shakespeare Milton and Donne* (Ann Arbor, Michigan, 1926), pp. 89–163: A. H. Gilbert, "Milton and Galileo", *S.P.*, XIX (1922), pp. 152–185; *"Milton's Textbook of Astronomy"*, *P.M.L.A.*, XXXVIII (1923), 297–307; "The Outside Shell of Milton's World", *S.P.*, XX (1923), pp. 444–447: E. N. S. Thompson, "Milton's Knowledge of Geography", *S.P.*, XVI (1919), pp. 148–171.

10. I. Langdon, *Milton's Theory of Poetry and the Fine Arts* (New Haven, 1924): K. Hartwell, *Lactantius and Milton* (Camb., Mass., 1929): H. Fletcher, *The Use of the Bible in Milton's Prose* (Urbana, Illinois, 1929).

11. E. E. Stoll, *Poets and Playwrights* (Minnesota, 1930).

12. W. Haller [ed.], *Tracts on Liberty in the Puritan Revolution, 1638–47* (New York, 1934).

13. G. C. Taylor, *Milton's Use of Du Bartas* (Camb., Mass., 1934).

14. W. Haller, *The Rise of Puritanism* (New York, 1938): A. Barker, *Milton and the Puritan Dilemma* (Toronto, 1942): A. S. P. Woodhouse, "Milton and His Age", *U.T.Q.*, V (1935), pp. 130–39; "Milton, Puritanism and Liberty", *U.T.Q.*, IV (1935), pp. 483–513; *Puritanism and Liberty* [ed. A. S. P. W.], (London, 1938), Intro. pp. 11–100: W. K. Jordan, *The Development of Religious Toleration in England* (London, 1932–40): G. W. Whiting, *Milton's Literary Milieu* (Chapel Hill, 1939): D. M. Wolfe, *Milton in the Puritan Revolution* (New York, 1941); *Leveller Manifestoes of the Puritan Revolution* [ed. D. M. W.], (New York, 1944), Intro. pp. 1–108: M. Y. Hughes, "Milton as a Revolutionary", *ELH*, IX (1943), pp. 87–116.

15. W. Haller, "Before Areopagitica", *P.M.L.A.*, XLII (1927), pp. 875–900; *Tracts on Liberty* [ed. W. H.], vol. I, pp. 128–39: W. R. Parker, *Milton's Contemporary Reputation* (Columbus, Ohio, 1940).

16. G. McColley, *Paradise Lost* (Chicago, 1940): A. Williams, "Milton and the Renaissance Commentaries on *Genesis*", *S.P.*, XXXIV (1937), pp. 191–208; "Renaissance Commentaries on *Genesis* and some elements of the theology of *Paradise Lost*", *P.M.L.A.*, LVI (1941), pp. 151–64; "Politics and Economics in Renaissance Commentaries on *Genesis*", *Huntingdon Library Quarterly*, VII (1944), pp. 207–22; "The Motivation of Satan's Rebellion in *Paradise Lost*", *S.P.*, XLII (1945), pp. 253–69: K. Svendsen, "Milton and the Encyclopaedias of Science", *S.P.*, XXXIX (1942), pp. 303–27; "Cosmological Lore in Milton", *ELH*, IX (1942), pp. 198–223 : A. O. Lovejoy, "Milton and the Paradox of the Fortunate Fall", *ELH*, IV (1937), pp. 161–79:

L. B. Campbell, "The Christian Muse", *Huntingdon Library Bulletin*, October, 1935, pp. 29–70: W. C. Curry, "Milton and the Scale of Nature", *Stanford University Studies in Language and Literature*, 1941, pp. 173–92.

17. M. H. Nicholson, "Milton and the Telescope", *ELH*, II (1935), pp. 1–32; "The Telescope and Imagination", *M.P.*, XXXII (1935), pp. 233–60; "The 'New Astronomy' and English Literary Imagination", *S.P.*, XXXII (1935), pp. 428–62: G. McColley, "The Astronomy of *Paradise Lost*", *S.P.*, XXXIV (1937), pp. 209–47; "Milton's Dialogue on Astronomy: The Principal Immediate Sources", *P.M.L.A.*, LII (1937), pp. 728–62: D. T. Starnes and E. W. Talbert, "John Milton and Renaissance Dictionaries", *Texas Studies in English* (1943), pp. 50–65: G. W. Whiting, *Milton's Literary Milieu* (Chapel Hill, 1939), pp. 94–128, 218–41.

18. W. R. Parker, *Milton's Debt to Greek Tragedy in Samson Agonistes* (Baltimore, 1937): M. Y. Hughes, "The Christ of *Paradise Regained* and the Renaissance Heroic Tradition", *S.P.*, XXXV (1938), pp. 254–77.

19. Dryden, "Dedication of the *Aeneis*", *Essays of John Dryden*, ed. W. P. Ker (Oxford, 1926), vol. I, p. 154. For a compact account of the status of the heroic poem in the seventeenth century see B. Willey, *The Seventeenth Century Background* (London, 1934), ch. x.

20. *Gabriel Harvey's Marginalia*, edited G. C. Moore Smith (Stratford-upon-Avon, 1913), pp. 160–61.

21. *Ibid.*, pp. 162–63.

22. Ben Jonson, "Timber or Discoveries", *Critical Essays of the Seventeenth Century*, edited J. E. Spingarn (Oxford, 1908), vol. I, p. 28: Milton, "Reason of Church Government", *Works, ed cit.*, vol. III, p. 239 and p. 241.

23. For evidence see *supra*, n. 22 and Vernon Hall, *Renaissance Literary Criticism* (New York, 1945), pp. 66 ff., p. 148 and pp. 218–19.

24. Comenius, *A Reformation of Schooles* (London, 1642).

NOTES TO "'PARADISE LOST' AND THE 'DE DOCTRINA CHRISTIANA'"

1. The chief theories regarding the dating of the "De Doctrina" are as follows:

(1) Before 1641, e.g., Rev. A. D. Barber, *Bibliotheca Sacra*, XVI (1859), pp. 557–603; XVII (1860). This is vitiated by the fact

that Milton holds Trinitarian views in 1629 (*Nat. Ode*, 8–14) and in 1641 ("Of Reformation", *Works, ed. cit.*, vol. III, p. 76). He is also Calvinist in 1645 ("The Doctrine and Discipline of Divorce", *Works, ed. cit.*, vol. III, pp. 440–41), but Arminian in the treatise and in *Paradise Lost*. Therefore if we accept Barber's view Milton was a Trinitarian in 1629, an Arian and an Arminian subsequently, a Trinitarian again in 1641, a Calvinist in 1645 and in the 1660's an Arminian with questionable beliefs in the Trinity.

(2) Between 1643 and 1645. This view is held by H. G. Rosedale (*Milton Memorial Lectures, 1908*, London, 1909, pp. 109–90). The positive arguments are dubious, and the Remonstrant sentiments of the Treatise cannot be reconciled to the Calvinist views held at this time by Milton.

(3) *Circa* 1660. Hanford, Sewell and Kelley are holders of this theory. The evidence on which it rests is as follows:

(1) The statement of the anonymous biographer;
(2) The inference, from the state of the present MS., that the original MS. was written by Jeremie Picard;
(3) The conclusion (J. H. Hanford, "The Date of Milton's *De Doctrina Christiana*", *S.P.*, XVII, 1920, pp. 309–19) that Picard was Milton's sole amanuensis from *ca.* 1658 to *ca.* 1660;
(4) The fact that this dating can be made consistent with what we know of Milton's theological views.

The first fourteen chapters of the manuscript now in the Public Record Office are in Skinner's hand. The remaining chapters have been revised by Skinner, Sumner and several amanuenses. The crucial question therefore arises whether the manuscript we know is doctrinally identical with the original draft by Picard, now dated contemporaneously with *Paradise Lost*. Sewell contends that it is not. His contention is that the Treatise went through three recensions. The Public Record manuscript is the third: the Picard draft is the second, and the two differ substantially in dogma. Hence the manuscript we know, does not give us Milton's beliefs at the time he wrote *Paradise Lost*. Sewell's argument includes the following contentions: (1) The Dedication supports a theory of recensions ("Milton's *De Doctrina Christiana*", *E.S.E.A.*, XIX, 1934, pp. 41 ff.); (2) The third book of *Paradise Lost* and especially lines 139–40, 245–49, 305–7, contain Trinitarian views on the Son (*Ibid.*, pp. 49–50; *A Study in Milton's Christian Doctrine*, London, 1939, pp. 86–88); (3) In the chapters in Skinner's hand there remain traces of earlier, more orthodox views (*Essays and Studies*, pp. 52–3); (4) In the chapters *not* in Skinner's hand there is only one explicitly Arian statement.

This was written not by Picard but by a later amanuensis and argues a relatively late shift to anti-Trinitarianism (*Ibid.*, p. 51). Naturally this cannot be taken as a fair statement of Sewell's argument, for which I must refer the reader to the originals. Maurice Kelley's *This Great Argument* (Princeton, 1941) is a very thorough examination of the available evidence. Its conclusions which I accept are (1) that there is no difference in dogma between the early and late books of *Paradise Lost*; (2) That the evidence for recensions is not conclusive; (3) That the Public Record manuscript does not differ in dogma from the draft by Picard; (4) That the Treatise and the Epic are doctrinally identical.

2. The theory that creation, for Milton, took place through God's withdrawal from Chaos, is based by Saurat on *Paradise Lost*, VII, 166–73 (*Milton, Man and Thinker*, London, 1944, pp. 102 ff., 236–38). In opposition, see G. C. Taylor, *Milton's Use of Du Bartas*, Camb., Mass., 1934, pp. 38–42; A. Sewell, *A Study in Milton's Christian Doctrine*, pp. 124–34, and in controversy with Saurat in *R.E.S.*, XV (1939), pp. 73–80, and Maurice Kelley, *op. cit.*, pp. 80–82, 209–12. Taylor, Sewell, and Kelley hold the opposite opinion to Saurat, i.e., that God is passively present in Chaos, and that Creation is an expansion of his area of activity, a putting forth and not a retraction of goodness.

In connection with III, 183–4, see Kelley, "The Theological Dogma of *Paradise Lost*, III, 173–202", *P.M.L.A.*, LII (1937), pp. 75–79. The theory of sexual creation depends on giving a forced meaning to "play", in a complicated passage from "Tetrachordon" (*Works, ed. cit.*, vol. IV, p. 85) and in *Paradise Lost*, VII, 8–12. See Saurat, *op. cit.*, pp. 240–41, and in opposition C. S. Lewis (*A Preface to Paradise Lost*, London, 1942, p. 83) and M. Kelley (*op. cit.*, pp. 128–30).

3. See *P.L.*, V, 117–118. "Evil into the mind of God and Man / May come and go." Saurat (*op. cit.*, p. 110) suggests the reading that I have mentioned. But God very probably means Angel. See T. H. Banks, "The Meaning of God in *Paradise Lost*", *M.L.N.*, LIV (1939), pp. 450–54, also the following from the "De Doctrina", which Milton elaborates with proof texts: "The name of God seems to be attributed to Angels, because as heavenly messengers they bear the appearance of the divine glory and speak in the very words of the Deity."

4. See Boethius, *De Cons. Phil.*, V, Pros. 6; Augustine, *De Civ. Dei*, XI, VI: Browne, *Rel. Med.*, I, XI (all quoted C. S. Lewis, *op. cit.*, p. 84) and Farrar, *History of Interpretation* (London, 1885), p. 143. Du Bartas wavers on this issue. Milton says nothing in the Treatise on the matter and, furthermore, he seems to contradict

himself in VIII, 227 ff., where it turns out that Raphael was absent on the last day of an "instantaneous" creation.

5. Kelley, *op. cit.*, *passim*; Keightley, *An Account of the Life, Opinions and Writings of John Milton* (London, 1855), p. 158: Barber, *Bibliotheca Sacra*, XVIII, pp. 28–34: M. A. Larson, "Milton and Servetus", *P.M.L.A.*, XLI (1926), pp. 891–934: Sewell, *A Study of Milton's Christian Doctrine*, and Sir H. J. C. Grierson, *Milton and Wordsworth* (Cambridge, 1938), p. 98.

6. *The Poetical Works of John Milton*, ed. H. J. Todd (London, 1842), vol. I, p. 196.

7. *Ibid.*, vol. I, p. 196.

8. *Ibid.*, vol. I, p. 199.

9. *Ibid.*, vol. I, p. 193. Johnson also argues that the poet appears "to have been untainted by any heretical peculiarity of opinion". *Lives of the English Poets*, ed. G. B. Hill, I, 155.

10. *Todd, ed. cit.*, vol. I, p. 203. Compare the *Quarterly Magazine*'s review of the Treatise: "knowing his opinion to be adverse to that which has almost universally prevailed throughout Christendom [he] was determined to adhere to the very language of scripture, so that both he and his readers might be able to affix their meanings to his verses." Also Grierson, *M.L.R.*, 1944, p. 99: "using thus the very words of scripture Milton is able to tell his story without a challenge to the orthodox of his day."

11. *Blackwood's* reviewer remarks that Milton's sins against orthodoxy in *Paradise Lost* "are those of omission not commission". *P.R.* is ruined by his dissimulation in suppressing any assertion of the divinity of the Son. See Menaka, "The Critical Reception of Milton's *De Doctrina Christiana*", *Texas Studies in English*, 1943, pp. 142–4, to which I am also indebted in my previous note.

12. *Todd, ed. cit.*, vol. I, pp. 193–4.

13. The point is Sewell's (*op. cit.*, p. 88).

14. See VIII, 419–21:

> No need that thou
> Should'st propagat already infinite
> And through all numbers absolute though one.

Kelley says this is explicitly Arian (*op. cit.*, pp. 120–21). Morris (*A Vindication of John Milton*, London, 1862, p. 62) cites it as a Trinitarian text. Barber assumes that the Son is being addressed and concludes that the passage is orthodox. Hartwell (*Lactantius and Milton*, Camb., Mass., 1929, pp. 93–96) quotes Lactantius to maintain that Milton's Deity is sexless. I think a Renaissance audience could have followed Barber. See, e.g., Simon Goulart trans. T. Lodge, *A Learned Summary of Du Bartas* (London, 1637), vol. II, p. 29: "The poet's opinion is that Adam in the Garden

conferred with our Lord. . . . And that which is said that we shall
see God face to face, hath no relation to his Essence. . . . But this
has relation to Jesus Christ the Sonne of God, manifested in the
flesh." It is also worth noting that in the tenth book it is the Son
who judges Adam and Eve. He is referred to as God (X, 101; X,
171) and as the Lord God (X, 163) and it is implied in X, 115–
23 that he has previously conversed with Adam in the Garden.

15. *Works, ed. cit.,* vol. XV, pp. 21–23.
16. *P.L.,* V, 469–76. In interpreting "forms" cp. Spenser "For of the
soul the body form doth take / For soul is form and doth the body
make", *An Hymn in Honour of Beauty,* st. xix.
17. *The Elizabethan World Picture* (London, 1943), p. 30.
18. See, e.g., Spenser, *Hymn of Heavenly Beauty,* st. vii.
19. Raleigh, Du Bartas, Purchas and Mercator all agreed that first
matter created *ex nihilo* was analogous to Chaos. Mercator's first
matter comprehends "all the forms of things, substances and
qualities, secretly within her bowels and intrinsick essence".
(Whiting, *Milton's Literary Milieu,* Chapel Hill, 1939, ch. I). See
also J. Swan, *Speculum Mundi* (Cambridge, 1643), pp. 42 ff., 71 ff.
According to Origen, Bonaventure and the author of the
Wonders of the Sacred Scripture (then attributed to Augustine) the
substance of men and angels is the same (McColley, *Paradise Lost,*
Chicago, 1940, pp. 72–73). Danaeus however drew a distinction
between earthly and heavenly matter (Whiting, *loc. cit.*). On
Milton's Angelology see C. S. Lewis, *op. cit.,* ch. XV.
20. However cp. Goulart: "And if the first matter had been of itselfe,
it should be equall with God, which no man dare ever thinke. It
hath then bin from some other than from itselfe: It is from God
or from some other before itselfe; but *there is but one onely
principall Creator which is God, the soveraigne and first being, from
whence all other proceede.* Shee is therefore of him: if of him shee is
as of his cause efficient: that is by generation and production
from his substance or by creation according to his mighty will,
without precede(n)t matter but of Nothing properly called
Nothing. The first matter then hath beene made of nothing in
time by the Eternall God" (*op. cit.,* pt. I, p. 15. My italics).
21. *Works, ed. cit.,* vol. XV, p. 229 and p. 219.
22. *Paradise Lost,* X, 789–92. Kelley (*op. cit.,* pp. 154–55 and pp.
31–32) also takes III, 245–49 as referring to the Mortalist heresy.
This is in opposition to Sewell (*E.S.E.A.,* 1934, pp. 49–50) who
takes it as referring to the theological question of whether or not
Christ yielded to death in his divine nature. The similarity of
phrasing between "all that of me can die" (III, 246) and "All of
me then shall die" (X, 792) supports Kelley. But the differences
are as important as the similarities. X, 792 is from a perplexed,

fallen and bewildered Adam and can therefore be openly mor
talist. III, 246 is something said by the Son and the question of a
death of the soul is left open. It should be noted that *Ps.* xvi. 10 and
Acts ii. 27, 28, 31, which are embodied in III, 245-49 are used by
Milton as mortalist texts (*Works, ed. cit.*, vol. XV, p. 231). But
Milton's readers would not have taken them thus. The equivo-
cating "All that of me can die" would be read as referring to the
orthodox belief that Christ did not suffer a death of the soul.

  For further comment on these passages see Saurat, *R.E.S.*, XII
(1936), pp. 323-24; Sewell, *R.E.S.*, XV (1939), pp. 73-75 and
Saurat's rejoinder, *ibid.*, pp. 78-80.

23. *Works, ed. cit.*, vol. XVI, pp. 113, 125, 133. Sewell argues
("Milton and the Mosaic Law", *M.L.R.*, XXX, 1935, pp. 13-
18, 218) that this passage does not square with the tenth chapter
of the Treatise, that Milton is undecided on the relationship of
the Law to the Gospel in *A Treatise of Civil Power in Ecclesiastical
Causes*, and that consequently his views on the subject were not
fully formed till after 1659. These contentions are fully refuted
by Kelley (*op. cit.*, pp. 56-67). Professor Arthur Barker ("Christian Liberty in Milton's Divorce Pamphlets", *M.L.R.*, XXXV,
1940, pp. 153-61) goes considerably further and suggests that
Milton, when he wrote *Tetrachordon*, had made up his mind on
the subject. He supports this with an analysis of the additions
made to later editions of *The Doctrine and Discipline of Divorce*.
I accept Kelley's conclusions but am not convinced by Barker's.

24. *Paradise Lost*, XII, 300-306. Professor Sewell argues (*op. cit.*) that
this passage expresses the same view as the twenty-sixth and
twenty-seventh chapters of the "De Doctrina".

25. *Vide Infra* pp. 159-60, n. 28 for documentation.

26. *Paradise Lost*, V, 600 ff.

27. *Paradise Lost*, V, 835-38. Cp. also II, 383-91.

28. Grierson, *op. cit.*, p. 99.

29. In the passage following Grierson's quotation Milton warns us
against this kind of inference. ". . . many commentators have
applied the passages which allude to the exaltation and mediatorial functions of Christ as proof of his generation from all
eternity. They have indeed this excuse, if any excuse can be
received in such a case, that it is impossible to find a single text
in all scripture to prove the eternal generation of the Son."
Works, ed. cit., vol. XIV, p. 181.

30. The loci of the controversy are Saurat, *Milton, Man and Thinker*,
pp. 173-74; Grierson, *M.L.R.*, XXI (1926), pp. 440-42; Grierson, *Milton and Wordsworth*, pp. 98-99; Saurat, *R.E.S.*, XIV
(1938), pp. 225-28; Grierson, *ibid.*, pp. 458-60 and Kelley, *op.
cit.*, pp. 94-106. Annotation has also been provided by H. F.

Fletcher (*Milton's Rabbinical Readings*, Urbana, 1930, pp. 150–55), by K. Hartwell (*op. cit.*, pp. 100–104) and by M. Y. Hughes in his edition of *Paradise Lost* (New York, 1935). Saurat interprets the passage literally, justifying its contradiction of V, 833–38 as a dramatic necessity. Grierson interprets figuratively and points out that the passage is not necessarily Arian. Hartwell, Fletcher and Hughes interpret the passage as suggesting that God created all things in the beginning, but that their natures only became manifest at various points in time. The sources of this idea are said to be rabbinical. Kelley treats the passage as one in which Biblical texts referring to the exaltation are transferred for dramatic reasons to the beginnings of celestial history. Hence the lines cannot be read as evidence for, or against, Milton's Arianism. The Treatise however is useful in defining Milton's special usage of the word "begot".

31. The point is Kelley's (*op. cit.*, p. 97). Grierson (*M.L.R.*, April, 1944) accepts it though he attributes it to Barker. But the displacement of these texts seems to have been first noted by Defoe: "Christ is declar'd the *Son of God with Power*, only by the resurrection of the dead, and this is both a Declaration in Heaven and Earth. Rom. i. 4. And *Milton* can have no authority to tell us, there was any declaration of it in Heaven before this, except it be that dull authority, call'd *poetic License*, which will not pass in so solemn an affair as that." *The Political History of the Devil* (London, 1726), p. 74.

32. *Works, ed. cit.*, vol. XV, p. 105. For further discussion see *supra* pp. 146–47 n. and p. 48

33. *Works, ed. cit.*, vol. XV, p. 111.

34. *supra* p. 70 and p. 155 n. for further discussion.

35. *De Doctrina Christiana, Works, ed. cit.*, vol. XV, p. 113. *Infra* p. 155 n. for further discussion.

36. *The Early Lives of Milton*, ed. H. Darbishire (London, 1932), p. 73 and p. 13.

37. The need for some such beginning was recognized by Defoe: "The thing was necessary to Milton who wanted to assign some cause or original of the *Devil's* rebellion; and so, as I said above, the design is well laid out, it only wants two Trifles call'd *Truth* and History." *Op. cit.*, p. 74. Professor McColley (*Paradise Lost*, Chicago, 1940, pp. 32–33) seems to wish to account for Milton's "design" by claiming a number of literary precedents for it. He asserts that "during Milton's era, the belief that the Exaltation (and Incarnation) occasioned Satan's rebellion enjoyed appreciable literary prestige" and appears to claim that this belief was adopted by Milton in the fifth book. But the Incarnation is revealed to the Angels in the third and not the fifth book of the

epic. Milton's motivation therefore seems to have no real precedent and so cannot be justified on this score, even if we assume (as I do not) that precedents provide sufficient reason for the adoption of a given device in a poem. So *Paradise Lost*, V, 600 ff. can only be defended, if at all, on the poetic grounds which I have tried to supply in this chapter. Such a defence would be in harmony with my several illustrations (*supra* pp. 48–50 and p. 155, n.8) of the way in which Milton departs from precedent when it does not happen to serve his poetic intention.

38. The theory is discussed by Z. S. Fink, "Milton and the Theory of Climatic Influence", *M.L.Q.*, 1941, pp. 67–80. Mr. Fink cites the exordium to the ninth book but does not seem to notice its lack of agreement with Phillips's testimony.

39. *Works, ed. cit.*, vol. XV, pp. 33–35.

40. *Works, ed. cit.*, vol. XVI, pp. 373–75.

41. Peter Heylyn, *The Summe of Christian Theologie* (London, 1673), pp. 112–13.

42. The unorthodoxy of Milton's cosmography seems to have escaped even a scholar as acute as Professor Dover Wilson: "Shakespeare inhabited the diminutive, compact and tidy universe designed by Ptolemy fifteen hundred years before his day, and his very language is full of astronomical notions now long forgotten. This universe was a miracle of ordered harmony. A 'pendent world', which included the whole starry space visible to man together with the containing Firmament, it hung like a jewel from the floor of Heaven, Hell lying beneath it and chaos about it." (*The Essential Shakespeare*, Cambridge, 1932, p. 15). Professor Wilson's version of the universe Shakespeare inhabited is based on Milton's cosmography, though I am not at all sure what he means by "firmament". The typical Elizabethan diagram however would be much more likely to show Hell in the centre of the earth which in turn would be the centre of a finite "world" surrounded by an infinite "empyrean". Milton therefore is being decidedly unusual in giving us a picture of the world with "Hell lying beneath it and chaos about it".

"PARADISE LOST": NOTES TO SECTION I

1. A great deal has been written on the subject. But see especially G. McColley, "Paradise Lost", *Harvard Theological Review*, XXXIII (1939), pp. 181–235.

2. Maury Thibaut de Maisières, *Les Poêmes inspirés du Début de la Genèse à l'Époque de la Renaissance* (Louvain, 1931), pp. 13–17.

3. P. E. Dustoor, "Legends of Lucifer in Early English and in Milton", *Anglia*, LIV (1930), pp. 213–268.
4. Dustoor, *op. cit.*, pp. 214–219, 254 ff. In the *Lyff of Adam and Eve* the Angels are created on the first day and fall on the sixth. Aquinas considers it probable that the Angels fell in the moment of their creation (*Summa Theologica*, Pt. 1, Q. LXIII, Art. 6). The Caedmonian Genesis is therefore exceptional in dating the fall of the Angels before the Creation.
5. Langland in *The Vision of Piers Plowman*, however, hits on Milton's nine.
6. Thibaut de Maisières, *op. cit,*, pp. 18–19.
7. For details see Arnold Williams, "Commentaries on *Genesis* as a basis for Hexaemeral Literature", *S.P.*, XXXIV (1937), pp. 191–208.
8. For evidence see Williams, "Milton and the Renaissance Commentaries on *Genesis*", *Modern Philology*, XXXVII (1939–40), pp. 263–78, and "Renaissance Commentaries on *Genesis* and some Elements of the Theology of *Paradise Lost*", *P.M.L.A.*, LVI (1941), pp. 151–64.
9. Thibaut de Maisières, *op. cit.*, p. 119.
10. McColley, *op. cit.*, pp. 184–85. But, in listing the ancient Fathers whom Milton could have quoted, Professor McColley does not make it clear that Milton's contemporaries and near contemporaries were solidly against him. I have consulted eleven of them and only one (Peter Heylyn) believes that the Angels were created before the world. I think this helps to account for the apologetic tone of the argument to the first book of *Paradise Lost*.
11. Some of the material I am using in the following paragraphs can be found in E. M. W. Tillyard, *Milton* (London, 1930), pp. 247–48: Charles Williams, *Reason and Beauty in the Poetic Mind* (Oxford, 1933), p. 122 n.: Tillyard, "The Causeway from Hell to the World in the Tenth Book of *Paradise Lost*", *S.P.*, XXXVIII (1941), pp. 266–70 and Maurice Kelley, *This Great Argument* (Princeton, 1941), p. 193 n.
12. *Isaiah* xiv. 14. For further documentation see McColley, *op. cit.*, pp. 185–86 n.
13. The mountain of the congregation is mentioned in *Isaiah* xiv. 13.
14. Milton's verses echo *Genesis* iii. 22. Calvin (*Commentary on Genesis*, chap. III, sect. 22) calls this an ironic comment. Andrew Willet (*Hexapla in Genesin*, London, 1632, p. 23) says that God, in saying that man has become like himself, "derideth man's folly". So Milton's harshness may, after all, be impersonal.
15. See A. O. Lovejoy, "Milton and the Paradox of the Fortunate Fall", *ELH*, IV (1937), pp. 161–79 and McColley, *op. cit.*, pp. 204–05.

16. For the idea that the permission of evil and its direction to good ends is a feature of God's Providence, see Henry Lawrence, *An History of Angells* (London, 1649) p. 68; Thomas Sutton, *Lecture upon the Eleventh Chapter to the Romans* (London, 1632) pp. 208 ff., Elnathan Parr, *The Grounds of Divinitie* (London, 1636), p. 202; Johan Wolleb, *Abridgment of Christian Divinitie*, translated and revised by Alexander Ross (London, 1660), p. 58, and John Davies of Hereford, "Mirum in Modum", *Works*, ed. Grosart (London, 1878), vol. I, p. 30.

17. The Scriptural Sanction is from 1 *Cor.* xv, 45 and *Rom.* v. 14. See also Calvin, *Institutes of the Christian Religion*, Bk. I, ch. xv, sect. 3–4; Donne, "Hymne to God my God in my Sicknesse", *Poetical Works*, ed. Sir H. J. C. Grierson (London, 1912), vol. I, p. 368; Thomas Goodwin, *Christ Set Forth* (London, 1642), pp. 82 ff.: Andrew Willet, *Hexapla* (London, 1616), pp. 256–58; Samuel Purchas, *loc. cit.*, *infra* n. 19, and W. Haller, *The Rise of Puritanism* (New York, 1938), ch. iv.

18. There is no scriptural text to support this. See however Crashaw, "The Himn O Gloriosa Domina", *Poetical Works*, ed. L. C. Martin (London, 1927), pp. 302–03, and John Swan, *Speculum Mundi* (Cambridge, 1643), pp. 497–98. Professor Saurat points out (*Milton Man and Thinker*, London, 1944, p. 218) that Milton in *Of Prelatical Episcopacy* upbraids Irenaeus for saying something very similar.

19. The chief scriptural texts incorporated by Milton are *Rom.* v. 17-19; 1 *Cor.* xv. 22; *Rom.* xi. 16; *John* xv. 25; *Gal.* ii. 20; 1 *Cor.* xi. 3 and *Col.* i. 18. Milton's elaboration of these texts is supported by Samuel Purchas, *Purchas His Pilgrim. Microcosmus or the Historie of Man* (London, 1627), pp. 150–52, 402–06, 676–78 and 777–82; by Elnathan Parr, *op. cit.*, pp. 321–22 and by the comment on *Rom.* v. 14 in *Annotations upon all the Books of the Old and New Testament . . . by the labour of Certain Divines thereunto appointed and therein employed* (London, 1651), vol. II. Hereafter cited as *Assembly Annotations*.

20. My interpretation modifies that of Professor McColley, who states (*Paradise Lost*, Chicago, 1940, p. 22) that, while early theologians interpreted *Rev.* xi. 7–9, as naming Michael as the conqueror of Satan, some altered the punctuation so that Christ could be regarded as intervening after Michael and Satan had waged an indecisive conflict. This may be true of patristic exegesis but my impression is that commentators in the seventeenth century identified Michael with Christ. See e.g., George Giffard, *Sermons upon the Whole Booke of the Revelation* (London, 1599), p. 228; William Cowper, "A Commentary upon the Revelation of St. John", *Works* (London, 1629), p. 1023; John

Napier, *A Plaine Discoverie of the Whole Revelation of St. John* (Edinburgh, 1645), p. 150, and Wolleb-Ross, *op. cit.*, p. 63. Milton in the "De Doctrina" admits the authority of this version: "it is generally supposed that Michael is Christ." But he goes on to support his version in *Paradise Lost*: "But Christ vanquished the devil and trampled him under foot singly; Michael, the leader of the angels, is introduced in the capacity of a hostile commander waging war with the prince of the devils, the armies on both sides being drawn out in battle array, and separating after a doubtful conflict." (*Works*, *ed. cit.*, vol. XV, p. 105). Accordingly, I have accepted Milton's account of the received tradition from which he is departing and tried to explain the poetic significance of this departure. Admittedly it squares with his beliefs. But I think it is also important that it can be poetically justified.

21. McColley, "Milton's Battle in Heaven and Rupert of St. Heribert", *Speculum*, XVI (1941), pp. 230–35.

22. McColley, *Paradise Lost* (Chicago, 1940), pp. 158 ff. Marianna Woodhull (*The Epic of Paradise Lost*, New York, 1907, p. 43) notes that no parallel exists for the episode but she does very little to justify the addition.

23. In "Paradise Lost" (*Harvard Theological Review*, 1939, pp. 210–11 n.) McColley cites II, 347 ff., IV, 287 ff., IV, 420 ff., IV, 623 ff. and IV, 776 ff. as evidence that the tentative temptation occurred on the first day. None of these references strikes me as at all conclusive and the last of them seems to contradict McColley's theory. In IV, 778–79, the Cherubim are described as issuing from their "Ivorie Port" at the "accustomd hour". They could hardly be doing this if this were the first night of Adam and Eve's creation. Moreover if Adam and Eve were created on this day they should be celebrating their nuptials on the night of the tentative temptation. There is every indication that this cannot be so. The arguments against Professor McColley's chronology are further strengthened by Adam and Eve's accounts of their creation and by the evidence cited in Newton's note on IV, 449. So in the absence of any further supporting evidence, Professor McColley's time-scheme must be regarded as unacceptable.

24. This was noted *en passant* by Addison (Todd, *ed. cit.*, vol. I, p. 321). Bailey, who also sees the resemblance (*Milton*, London, 1915, p. 186) differs from me about its effect: ". . . we notice such things as Eve's dream in the fifth book which, anticipating as it does so many of the details of her temptation, renders her fall much less probable, and goes far to destroy its interest when it occurs."

"PARADISE LOST": NOTES TO SECTION II

1. *The Elizabethan World Picture* (London, 1943), p. 23.
2. *The Great Chain of Being* (Cambridge, Mass., 1936), *passim*.
3. *The Governor*, Bk. I, ch. vii.
4. *The Laws of Ecclesiastical Polity*, Bk. I, ch. xvi, sect. 8.
5. Quoted Tillyard, *op. cit.*, p. 94.
6. See Edward Reynolds, *A Treatise of the Passions* (London, 1640), p. 75.
7. *A Preface to Paradise Lost* (London, 1942), p. 72.
8. *Op. cit.*, Bk. I, ch. i.
9. Sir John Fortescue, *Works*, edited Lord Clermont (London, 1869), vol. I, p. 322. Quoted Tillyard, *op. cit.*, pp. 24–25.
10. *Historia Mundi*, Englished by W. S. (London, 1635), p. 25.
11. The idea is based on *Gen.* i. 26, and can be found in any Renaissance commentary on the text. More unusual is the belief that the image of God in man consists wholly or partly in his dominion over other creatures. See e.g., Reynolds, *op. cit.*, ch. xxxvi; Parr, *op. cit.*, p. 193, Ussher, *A Body of Divinitie* (London, 166), pp. 104–5 and *Paradise Lost*, VIII, 540–46.
12. See McColley, *Harvard Theological Review*, XXXII, pp. 201–202, for references to Hugo of St. Victor, Peter Lombard, and St. Bonaventure. Also Romei, *Courtier's Academy* (Englished by I. H., 1598), p. 47 and Hooker, *op. cit.*, Bk. I, ch. vi, sect. 1.
13. "A Tale of a Tub", *Prose Works*, ed. H. Davis (Oxford, 1939), vol. I, p. 55.
14. *Lives*, ed. G. B. Hill (Oxford, 1905), vol. I, p. 24.
15. See Masson's comment on *Paradise Lost* II, 1051–53.
16. A. O. Lovejoy, *op. cit.*, p. 165. The credit for shattering the walls of the Ptolemaic universe was subsequently claimed for Bruno. Later F. R. Johnson maintained that Thomas Digges "was the first modern astronomer of note to portray an infinite heliocentric universe with the stars scattered at varying distances throughout infinite space". *Astronomical Thought in Renaissance England* (Baltimore, 1937), pp. 164–65. A year before this, Professor McColley had argued that the theory of an infinite universe was definitely advocated by Copernicus. ("The Seventeenth Century Doctrine of a Plurality of Worlds", *Annals of Science*, I, 1936, pp. 385–430). Johnson (*op. cit.*, pp. 107–08 n.) rejects this contention. McColley repeats it with additional evidence in "The Universe of De Revolutionibus" (*Isis*, XXX, 1939, pp. 452–72).
17. John Eachard, *Grounds and Occasions of the Contempt of the Clergy and Religion* (London, 1670).

NOTES

"PARADISE LOST": NOTES TO SECTION III

1. *Purchas His Pilgrimage or Relations of the World* (London, 1613), p. 11. Hereafter cited as *Pilgrimage*.
2. Quoted C. S. Lewis, *op. cit.*, p. 113. For the idea see also Simon Goulart trans. Thomas Lodge, *A Learned Summary of Du Bartas* (London, 1637), pt. II, p. 18; Henry More, *Conjectura Cabbalistica*, p. 24 (Printed in *A Collection of Several Philosophical Writings*, London, 1662); Willet, *Hexapla in Genesin* (London, 1632), p. 30; Alexander Ross, *An Expositione on the Fourteene First Chapters of Genesis* (London, 1626), p. 51; John Salkeld, *A Treatise of Paradise* (London, 1613), p. 189 and Lancelot Andrewes, *A Collection of Posthumous and Orphan Lectures* (London, 1652), p. 212.
3. *Paradise Lost*, V, 100 ff. McColley (*op. cit.*, pp. 166–8) concludes that the passage is based on one in Phineas Fletcher's *Purple Island*. But similar poetic descriptions can be found in Davies's *Nosce Teipsum* and Fulke Greville's *Treatise of Human Learning*. Prose counterparts are too numerous to be worth citing but for a selection see K. Svendsen, "Milton and the Encyclopaedias of Science", *S.P.*, XXIX (1942).
4. Denis Saurat (*op. cit.*, pp. 264–65) quotes Fludd for the idea. But see also *Timon of Athens*, IV, iii. 433 ff.
5. P. L. Carver ("The Angels in Paradise Lost", *R.E.S.*, XVI, 1940, p. 417) here sees a possible allusion to a passage from Duns Scotus. But C. S. Lewis's explanation (*op. cit.*, p. 106) seems to me adequate. Nevertheless Milton's furious insistence on detail (Tasting, concoct, digest, assimilate / And corporeal to incorporeal turn) seemed to me inexplicable until I ran across the following in Peter Martyr's *Commonplaces*: "*Scotus* thinketh, that to eate, is nothing else but to chawe meate, and to conveie it downe into the bellie: but this did the Angels; wherefore he gathereth that they did verilie eate. Others thinke, that to eate, is not onelie to chawe the meate, or to conveie it downe into the bellie; but further to convert it to the substance of his own bodie, by concoction through the quickening power; which thing seeing the Angels did not, they did not trulie eate." (Trans. Anthony Marten, London, 1583, pt. I, p. 118). Milton is obviously arguing that the angels *did* eat in the second sense, and despite Mr. Lewis's citations and Mr. McColley's (*op. cit.*, p. 70), it still seems to me to be a drastic thing to say.
6. Robert Burton, *The Anatomy of Melancholy*, pt. I, sect. 1, memb. 11, subsect. 11.
7. Milton's statement that discursive and intuitive reason differ only in degree may seem extraordinary but I imagine it could be supported from Aquinas (*Summa Theologica*, pt. I, Q. LXXIX, art. 8. Trans. of the Fathers of the English Dominican Province):

". . . in the angels the power of knowledge is not of a different genus from that which is the human reason but is compared to it as the perfect to the imperfect." Milton uses the distinction with superb effect in II, 557 ff. where the fallen angels, *arguing* over fixed fate, free-will, and foreknowledge, do so only because they have lost their powers of intuitive apprehension.

Theodore Spencer (*Shakespeare and the Nature of Man*, London, 1943, p. 12 n.) argues that Milton in this passage is identifying understanding with common sense. This is a possible reading but it is incompatible with IX, 1121 ff. I think that Milton couples reason with understanding, possibly regarding them as active and passive aspects of the same faculty. Mainly on the evidence of IX, 113, I should conclude that Milton is following the Renaissance version of Aristotelian, rather than Platonic, psychology. Everything he says seems compatible with this version. But the matter is not really important. Milton's contemporaries were more muddled about the divisions than scholars like to think and Calvin's presentation (*Institutes*, Bk I, ch. xv, sects. 6–7) would hardly have enlightened them. What matters is not the accuracy with which such concepts are employed but the stock responses aroused by their employment.

8. The motif recurs in everything Raphael says. Cp. V, 522, V, 541, VI, 911, VIII, 634. Similarly Augustine argues that obedience is "the mother and guardian of all the other virtues of the soul". (*De Civ. Dei*, Trans. M. Dodds, Bk. XIV, ch. xii). William Perkins asserts that "the fall is a revolting of the reasonable creature from obedience to Sin." ("A Golden Chaine", *Works*, London, 1616, vol. I, p. 18.) Calvin concludes that "the prohibition of the tree of knowledge of good and evil was a test of obedience that Adam might prove his willing submission to the Divine Government". (*Institutes*, trans. J. Allen, Philadelphia, 1936, Bk. II, ch. i, sect. 4). Hooker therefore is more than justified in putting the question "see we not plainly that obedience of creatures unto the law of nature is the stay of the whole world?" (*Of the Laws of Ecclesiastical Polity*, I, iii, 2).

9. The classical authority for the idea is *Symposium*, 210–212, the scriptural *Rom*. i. 20. It is discussed by A. O. Lovejoy (*The Great Chain of Being*, Cambridge, Mass., 1936, pp. 89 ff.) and by W. C. Curry ("Milton and the Scale of Nature", *Stanford University Studies in Lang. and Lit.*, 1941, pp. 173–92). See among Milton's near contemporaries Spenser, *An Hymne of Heavenly Beauty*; Stafford, *Niobe* (London, 1611), p. 3; Goodman, *The Fall of Man* (London, 1616), pp. 152–3; John Smith, *Select Discourses* (London, 1660), pp. 430–1 and Henry Reynolds, "Mytho-

mestes", *Critical Essays of the Seventeenth Century*, ed. J. E. Spingarn, vol. I, p. 174.

10. The relation of the Symbolism of the dance to that of degree is discussed by E. M. W. Tillyard (*op. cit.*, pp. 94–99). Milton has already alluded to the cosmic dance in describing Satan's journey (III, 579 ff.) and in the morning prayer of Adam and Eve (V, 175 ff.). Paradise at IV, 264 ff. is described in similar language and even the Copernican System is visualized as a dance at VIII, 122 ff. The correspondence between the cosmic dance and the celestial suggested at V, 617 ff., is acknowledged by Satan at IX, 99 ff. It reinforces the analogy between earth and heaven which Raphael considers at V, 574 ff. This is further emphasized by the references to a heavenly Paradise at V, 500 and to the removal of amarant from Paradise to Heaven (III, 351 ff.). For the former see Henry Ainsworth, *Annotations upon the Five Bookes of Moses* (London, 1627), pp. 10–11; Alexander Ross, *An Exposition on the Fourteene First Chapters of Genesis* (London, 1626), p. 42; *Annotations upon all the Books of the Old and New Testament* (London, 1651), vol. I comment on *Genesis* ii. 9, and Edward Leigh, *A Systeme or Body of Divinitie* (London, 1654), p. 293. Leigh's comment is particularly striking. "Paradise was a little model of Heaven, and a sign of the great Heaven, assuring *Adam*, that if he continued in obedience to God, he should be translated into Heaven, to enjoy God supernaturally, as there he did enjoy him naturally." Milton adds to all this, his notion that man may dwell at option in earthly or celestial paradises. His story of the removal of amarant is probably also his own, though it is intended to allude to 1 *Pet.* i. 4 and 1 *Pet.* v. 4.

11. Dustoor (*op. cit., passim*) devotes much space to puzzling out the orders of Milton's angels. However I agree with Dr. Tillyard (*op. cit.*, p. 39) that Milton "has his various hierarchies but lays down no precise order". After all Calvin had asserted that "if we wish to be truly wise, we must forsake the vain imaginations propagated by triflers concerning the nature, orders, and multitude of angels. . . . No man can deny that great subtlety and acuteness is discovered by Dionysius, whoever he was, in many parts of his treatise on the celestial Hierarchy; but if any one enters into a critical examination of it, he will find the greatest part of it to be mere babbling." (*Institutes, ed. cit.*, Bk. I, ch. xiv, sect. 4). Or as Bucanus puts it: "But that there be Hierarchies, and degrees of Hierarchies among the Angels as the Papists imagine, it cannot be proved by any testimony of Scripture." (William Bucanus, *Institutes of Christian Religion*, trans. R. Hill, London, 1606, p. 69). See also James Ussher, *A Body of Divinitie*, 4th edn. (London, 1663), p. 116; Edward Leigh, *op. cit.*, p. 272,

and Samuel Purchas, *op. cit.*, p. 567. Milton was therefore quite justified in refusing to be exact and in using these angelic titles purely for the sake of their poetic evocations.

12. Quoted A. S. P. Woodhouse, *Puritanism and Liberty* (London, 1938), p. 201.

13. Cp. Woodhouse, *op. cit.*, Introduction p. 62: "Once the inferior magistrates have declared against the prince and freed opposition from the stigma of rebellion, so staunch a Calvinist as Rutherford can forge in *Lex Rex* almost every argument of revolution later to be employed by the Levellers."

14. *P.L.*, VI, 40–43 and I, 248–49. There are other phrases which are remembered in Hell. Compare V, 886–88, with II, 327–28, and VI, 183–84, with I, 263. The last two are noted by Todd and Newton.

15. G. Wilson Knight, *Chariot of Wrath* (London, 1942), p. 158.

16. G. McColley, *op. cit.*, pp. 45–47.

17. G. McColley, *op. cit.*, ch. iii.

18. G. McColley, "Milton's Dialogue on Astronomy: The Principal Immediate Sources", *P.M.L.A.*, LII (1937), pp. 728–62. The "immediate sources" are John Wilkins's *The Discovery of a World in the Moone* (3rd edn., London, 1640); *A Discourse concerning a New Planet* (London, 1640; bound with the 3rd edn. of the "Discovery" as a second part) and Alexander Ross's *The New Planet no Planet: or the Earth no Wandring Star* (London, 1646).

Much misunderstanding exists, especially in annotated editions of *Paradise Lost*, concerning the theories discussed in the dialogue on Astronomy. The received tradition is that the Ptolemaic and Copernican Systems were the reigning alternatives for Milton's generation, that the dialogue is devoted to discussing their respective merits, and that Milton, while preferring the latter, bases his cosmography, for poetic reasons, on the former. In fact, four distinct conceptions are discussed: the Copernican System, the Ptolemaic, the theory of a plurality of worlds and the idea of the diurnal rotation of the Earth. The last of these, usually thought of as part of the Copernican System, was often supported quite independently of it. Thus, among its advocates, William Gilbert ignores the heliocentric hypothesis, and Nathaniel Carpenter, Francis Godwin and Anthony Deusingius reject it. Diurnal rotation is discussed by Milton at five points in the dialogue (VIII, 13 ff.; 64 ff.; 85 ff.; 133 ff.; 160 ff.) and also at IV, 592 ff. At VIII, 133 ff. it seems to be proposed as an alternative to the Copernican hypothesis.

Another deficiency in the received explanation is its omission of the theory of the plurality of worlds. The history of the idea has been discussed by McColley (*Annals of Science*, I, 1936, pp.

385–430). Milton alludes to it in three forms: (1) that the moon may be like the earth and inhabited; (2) that other parts of the universe may be like the earth and inhabited; (3) that there may be other universes similar to ours. The place of (1) in seventeenth century thought has been discussed by Professor M. Nicholson ("A World in the Moon", *Smith College Studies in Modern Languages*, XVII, 2, 1936, pp. 36–44 *et passim*). Milton glances at it in I, 286 ff., is critical of it in V, 261–63, and noncommittal in the dialogue (VIII, 140 ff.). But in III, 459–62 (strangely ignored by commentators) he is more specific and takes the idea at least as seriously as he takes his limbo. (2) probably lies behind III, 667–70, and is touched on in III, 561 ff., and VII, 621–22, while (3) is discussed at some length in the dialogue (VIII, 148 ff.).

The received explanation is correct in stressing Milton's hostility to the Ptolemaic hypothesis. But it does not follow that he supports the Copernican. Since he neither accepts nor rejects the heliocentric theory and since there were alternative systems based on diurnal rotation he may have preferred Purchas's "learned ignorance" on these matters (*Pilgrimage*, 2nd ed., London, 1614, p. 10). The received explanation is also misleading when it implies that the Ptolemaic and Copernican hypotheses were the reigning alternatives for Milton's generation. It was the geo-heliocentric Tychonic System which was contending with the Copernican for supremacy; both in learned treatises and in popular almanacs opinion was divided fairly evenly between them. (F. R. Johnson, *op. cit.*, pp. 248–87: G. McColley, "The Astronomy of *Paradise Lost*", *S.P.*, XXXIV, 1937, pp. 210–11, 234–38). The Tychonic System is not mentioned in *Paradise Lost* and the omission greatly affects the value of the dialogue as a record of the opinions prevailing in Milton's generation.

To conclude it seems probable that Milton's knowledge of astronomy has been overestimated. McColley (*op. cit.*, pp. 232–34) points out that his version of the Copernican System was out of date and Johnson concludes (*op. cit.*, p. 285) that Milton's "scientific knowledge in such matters was probably inferior to Donne's, and certainly to Gabriel Harvey's". But one should also insist that the aim of the dialogue is not so much to decide between rival theories in astronomy as to decide to what extent such theories are worth while. The conclusion is that they are inconclusive, and that we are not to vex our thoughts "with matters hid" but to concentrate instead on the daily business of living. It is a verdict far from palatable to us, but it is argued too plainly to be otherwise interpreted.

19. William Perkins, "Of Christian Oeconomie or Household Government", *Works* (London, 1616), vol. III, p. 691.
20. Simon Goulart trans. Thomas Lodge, *op. cit.*, pt. I, p. 297.
21. Calvin, *Commentary on 1 Corinthians*, trans. Rev. John Pringle (Edinburgh, 1848), ch. xi, sect. 7. These quotations should make it clear that Milton's attitude to women is typical of his time. But see also Chilton Powell, *English Domestic Relations* (New York, 1917), p. 177 n. *et passim*; Louis B. Wright, *Middle Class Culture in Elizabethan England* (Chapel Hill, 1935), ch. vii and especially p. 204; M. M. Knappen, *Tudor Puritanism* (Chicago, 1940), pp. 451–55 and W. and M. Haller, "The Puritan Art of Love", *Huntingdon Library Quarterly*, V (1942), pp. 235–72.
22. *The Confessions of St. Augustine*, trans. F. J. Sheed (London, 1944), p. 287.
23. Browne, "Pseudodoxia Epidemica", *Works*, ed. Charles Sayle (London, 1904), vol. I, p. 125.

"PARADISE LOST": NOTES TO SECTION IV

1. Swan, *op. cit.*, p. 498.
2. Lines 157–67 of Satan's Soliloquy at this point are illuminated by this comment of Lancelot Andrewes: "And the fathers doe think that Almighty God of set purpose, did allot him this creature and restrain him all other, for these two respects: first, thereby to punish the pride and the ambitious nature of the Devill, that he might see and all the world perceive, to what his sinne of pride had brought him, because he which a little before was so vainglorious as to presume to exalt him in God's throne and be as God, is now cast down in most vile and miserable sort, basely and contemptibly crawling upon the ground and being as the abject and most hated worm on the earth." (*op. cit.*, p. 253).
3. Perhaps Milton took the idea from Rabbinical sources. See Louis Ginzberg, *Legends of the Jews* (Philadelphia, 1909), vol. I, pp. 25–26.
4. Verity in his edition of *Paradise Lost* (London, 1936, p. 572) notes the resemblance to Areopagitica.
5. For catalogues of sins which are included in the sin of Adam and Eve see Milton, "De Doctrina Christiana", *Works, ed. cit.*, vol. XV, pp. 181–183; Augustine, *Enchiridion*, ch. xlv; Downame, *op. cit.*, pp. 233–34; Bucanus, *op. cit.*, p. 160; Leigh, *op. cit.*, p. 304; Ussher, *op. cit.*, pp. 134–36; Parr, *op. cit.*, pp. 252–53, and Willet, *Hexapla in Genesin*, p. 47.
6. Godfrey Goodman, *op. cit.*, p. 429.

7. McColley, who cites Caedmon as a precedent, says (*op. cit.*, p. 174) that Milton's insistence on Eve's gluttony is unusual. But the following, from Goodman, matches Milton's treatment:

    "The first Sinnes of the mind seeme to be disobedience and pride. . . . And for our bodie, gluttonie seemes to be the wellspring of all our carnall and bodily Sinnes: as a surfeit it is for the most part the beginning of all our diseases, and whereunto man is most subject and prone: it doth undoubtedly argue that the first Sinne was the Sinne of a surfeite and gluttonie, the tasting of forbidden fruit."

    Furthermore Milton's insistence on this aspect of Eve's sin enables him to separate the visions of the eleventh book into a pageant of diseases proceeding from the "Inabstinence" of Eve and one of licentiousness proceeding from the uxoriousness of Adam.

8. McColley (*op. cit.*, p. 178) describes as distinctly uncommon the idea that there was lustful cohabitation in Paradise. The matter is not discussed in the *De Doctrina Christiana*. Plainly Milton intends to contrast this carnality with the purity and reasonableness of wedded love:

    > By thee adulterous lust was driven from men
    > Among the bestial herds to raunge, by thee
    > Founded in Reason, Loyal, Just and Pure
    > Relations dear, and all the Charities
    > Of Father, Son, and Brother first were known.

    Also unusual is Milton's description of the fruit as an intoxicant (IX, 793; IX, 837-38; IX, 1008 ff.; IX, 1046 ff.). The *De Doctrina Christiana* does not imply this. In fact, chapter ten suggests that the fruit had no powers of any kind. Of the fourteen other commentators I have consulted, the majority agree with the "De Doctrina", and none provide any encouragement for the version in *Paradise Lost*. So, if we were to take this version at its face value, it would run counter to tradition and also to what we know of Milton's beliefs. Hence I feel that it is simply a figure of speech, introduced in order to stress still more the gross physical aftermath of Sin and that Milton does not believe in the conceit or intend his audience to believe it.

9. Andrewes, *op. cit.*, pp. 255 ff.

10. Downame, *op. cit.*, p. 235.

11. G. Lawson, *A Body of Divinitie* (London, 1659), p. 63. On the Devil's rhetoric see also Ussher, *op. cit.*, p. 130. The serpent's claim to have attained knowledge by eating the fruit is also unusual. I have not come across it except in Beaumont's *Psyche* (Canto VI, stanzas 282-4).

12. *Paradise Lost*, VI, 780-84; VIII, 511-15; IX, 782-83; IX, 1000-1003. The idea is fairly frequent (see McColley, *op. cit.*, p. 174).

13. Purchas (*Microcosmus*, p. 226) embroiders on this sentiment. "Such indeed is the sympathie betwixt the Soule and Bodie, that as *Adam* and *Eve*, they will take part each with other, though it be in the forbidden fruit; both tempting and tempted of each other, living and dying together."

14. Milton claims (IX, 998–99) that Adam ate "Against his better knowledge, not deceav'd, / But fondly overcome with femal charm". It is a version supported by 1 *Tim.* ii. 14, and Augustine, *De Civ. Dei*, Bk. XII, ch. xi. Calvin (*Commentary on Genesis*, ch. iii, sect. 6) dislikes the opinion, but cites it as commonly received. Several theologians, following him, concluded that Adam was also deceived. See, e.g., Leigh, *op. cit.*, p. 304; Willet, *op. cit.*, p. 39 (misnumbered 29); and Gervase Babington, "Certaine Plaine Briefe and Comfortable Notes upon every Chapter of Genesis", *Works* (London, 1637), p. 16. It is difficult to say what Andrewes (*op. cit.*, pp. 285–6) thinks but he seems, on the whole, to support Milton's version.

15. "Reason of Church Government", *Works*, *ed. cit.*, vol. III, p. 276.

16. Edward Reynolds, *A Treatise of the Passions and Faculties of the Soul of Man* (London, 1640), p. 63.

17. Purchas, *Microcosmus*, p. 152.

18. Pierre Charron puts the situation as follows: "These are the Principal Winds that raise all the storms in our souls; and the Cavern (like that of Aeolus) where they are engender'd and from whence they break loose, is nothing else but opinion. . . . The Will is made by Nature to follow the directions of the Understanding; this is its Guide to instruct, its Candle to give it Light; but when once the strength of Passion hath corrupted, and, as it were laid violent Hands upon the Will, then the Will in like manner, corrupts, and commits a violence on the Understanding. . . . What was at first in the Sensual Appetite only, hath made its way higher and got the Upper Hand of the Understanding; what was merely Passion and Pleasure, hath been advanced into a Principle of Religion and an Article of Faith." (*Of Wisdom*, trans. G. Stanhope, London, 1727, vol. I, pp. 200, 171 and 173). The notion that the conformity of the sensitive appetite to reason was destroyed as a result of the Fall is fairly frequent and can be studied in Leigh, *op. cit.*, p. 579; Wolleb-Ross, *op. cit.*, pp. 71, 79–80; Edward Reynolds, *op. cit.*, p. 62–3; Aquinas and Daniel Dyke, *infra*, n. 19, n. 22; Browne, *Pseudodoxia Epidemica*, Bk. I, ch. i, and Burton, *The Anatomy of Melancholy*, pt. I, sect. 1, memb. 11, subsect. xi.

19. *Summa Theologica*, *ed. cit.*, pt. II, Q. CXLIV, art. 1.

20. Goodman, *op. cit.*, p. 17.

21. Calvin, *Commentary on Genesis*, Trans. J. King (Edinburgh, 1848), ch. iii, sect. 17.

22. Daniel Dyke, *Two Treatises. The One of Repentance, the Other of Christ's Temptation* (London, 1646), p. 235 (misnumbered 225). The way in which the depravity of man is mirrored in the Creation is described by Burton at the beginning of the "Anatomy" in Du Bartas's *The Furies* and by Goodman, *op. cit.*, p. 218.

23. Purchas, *Pilgrimage*, p. 23. Calvin's more prosaic version may also be quoted: "And his [Adam's] guilt, being the origin of that curse which extends to every part of the world, it is reasonable to conclude its propagation to all his offspring. Therefore, when the Divine Image in him was obliterated, and he was punished with the loss of wisdom, strength, sanctity, truth, and righteousness, with which he had been adorned, but which were succeeded by the dreadful pests of ignorance, impotence, impurity, vanity, and iniquity, he suffered not alone, but involved all his posterity with him, and plunged them into the same miseries." (*Institutes*, *ed. cit.*, Bk. II, ch. i, sect. 5).

24. According to Goodman: "It stood with the justice of God, that the woman first enticing and abusing her husband, should now incurre a thraldome, and be made a captive to the will of her great Lord and Master (her husband)." (*Op. cit.*, p. 250). Goodman adds characteristically "I know not whether I should call this just decree of God either a curse or a blessing". See also Willet, *op. cit.*, p. 49, and the Assembly's comment on *Gen.* iii. 16. Calvin on the same place is equally severe but Babington *op. cit.*, p. 18) and Andrewes (*op. cit.*, p. 314) are more humane.

25. G. W. Whiting, *op. cit.*, p. 121. The Atlas is Jansson's *Novus Atlas* published in eleven volumes apparently from 1647 to 1662. But according to Kester Svendsen ("Cosmological Lore in Milton", *ELH*, IX, 1942, pp. 208 ff.) an encyclopaedia will do almost as well as an Atlas.

26. Eve's admission—"both have sin'd, but thou / Against God onely, I against God and thee"—recalls this comment of Aquinas: ". . . the woman not only herself sinned, but suggested sin to the man; wherefore she sinned against both God and her neighbour." (*Summa Theologica, ed. cit.*, pt. II, Q. CLXIII, art. 4).

27. "Adam Unparadiz'd", *Works, ed. cit.*, vol. XVIII, pp. 231–32.

"PARADISE LOST": NOTES TO SECTION V

1. Patrick Hume, *Annotations of Milton's Paradise Lost* (London, 1695), p. 300.

2. Todd, *ed. cit.*, vol. I, p. 352.
3. Quoted Todd, *ibid.*, vol. I, p. 353.
4. C. S. Lewis, *op. cit.*, p. 125.
5. E. M. W. Tillyard, *Milton* (London, 1930), p. 291.
6. Sir H. J. C. Grierson, *Milton and Wordsworth* (Cambridge, 1937), pp. 120, 121. For further discussion of the pessimism of the last two books of *Paradise Lost* see G. W. Whiting, *op. cit.*, ch. iv; G. McCollcy, *op. cit.*, pp. 333–36; Arnold Williams, "Conservative Critics of Milton", *The Sewanee Review*, XLIX (1941), pp. 90 ff., and Malcolm Mackenzie Ross, *Milton's Royalism* (Ithaca, 1943), ch. iii.
7. G. W. Whiting, *op. cit.*, pp. 119–20.
8. Ussher, *op. cit.*, p. 143.
9. Goodman, *op. cit.*, p. 78.
10. Moore, *A Mappe of Mans Mortalitie* (London, 1617), p. 15.
11. Purchas, *Microcosmus*, ch. xxxii.
12. *Ibid.*, p. 273.
13. *Vide* McColley, *op. cit.*, ch. viii.
14. *Works, ed. cit.*, vol. III, p. 238.
15. *P.L.*, V, 582–83.
16. "Reason of Church Government", *Works, ed. cit.*, vol. III, p. 238.
17. *warfaring* instead of *wayfaring* is recommended by the Columbia editors.
18. For documentation see Lily B. Campbell, *Shakespeare's Tragic Heroes* (Cambridge, 1930), pp. 95 ff., and Antony Nixon, *The Dignitie of Man* (London, 1612), p. 79.
19. Willet, *op. cit.*, pp. 99–100; Calvin, *Commentary on Genesis, ed. cit.*, pp. 316–19; Babington, *op. cit.*, pp. 34–35; Assembly's comments on *Gen.* x. 8–10, and Nicholas Gibbens, *Questions and Disputations concerning the Holy Scripture* (London, 1602), p. 431.
20. *Works, ed. cit.*, vol. V, p. 1. One should add Milton's observation in *Tetrachordon* that commonwealths decay "when men cease to do according to the inward and uncompelled notions of virtue, caring only to live by the outer constraint of the law", (*Ibid.*, vol. IV, p. 137).
21. *Prose Works*, ed. J. A. St. John (London, 1848), vol. I, p. 298.
22. *P.R.*, IV, 143–45. See also *P.R.*, II, 466–80.
23. For the background of the idea see first and foremost Gierke, *Political Theories of the Middle Ages*, trans. F. W. Maitland (Cambridge, 1900), pp. 7–10, 101–103. More information is provided by George P. Conger, *Theories of Macrocosms and Microcosms in the History of Philosophy* (New York, 1922). Affiliations with Plato are dealt with by H. Agar in *Milton and Plato* (Princeton, 1928), and the Elizabethan correspondences discussed by E. M. W. Tillyard in *The Elizabethan World Picture*, pp. 82–93. One should

also note the resemblance of Milton's thought to that of Whichcote from whom I quote: "The *Government* of our Spirits is the
greatest *Freedom.* . . . Every *Mis-government* of ourselves is a
punishment of ourselves. . . . Man parts with his Freedom, and
enslaves himself; when he *subjects* himself to That, which is not
Sovereign in him; as *Reason* is. . . . *Good men*, under the Power of
Reason and Religion, are *Free*; in the worst Condition: *Badmen*,
under the Power of Lust and Vice, are *Slaves*; in the best Condition . . . *True* Liberty, as well as power, is always in conjunction
with Right and Good. It is Licentiousness and weakness, that
are separated from it. . . . The government of Man *should be* the
Monarchy of Reason; it *is* too often a Democracy of Passions or
Anarchy of Humours." (*Moral and Religious Aphorisms*, Nos. 62,
80, 239, 294, 383, 479). Cf. also John Smith's reference to
"Liberty which is founded in Reason, and which Mankind only
in this lower world hath above other Creatures". (*Select Discourses*, London, 1673, p. 284).

24. Cp. Whichcote, *Aphorisms*, No. 480: "Better have no Confidence,
than Self-Confidence."

25. *Works, ed. cit.*, vol. XVI, p. 101.

26. J. Weemse, *The Portraiture of the Image of God in Man*, (London,
1636), p. 64.

27. Goodman, *op. cit.*, p. 5.

28. As this relationship is not always understood I may be forgiven
for trying to outline it. The Mosaic Law is Ceremonial, Judicial,
and Moral. The rites performed under the Ceremonial Law are
types of the Messiah and are abolished by his coming. The
Judicial Law was ordained for the administration of the Jewish
Commonwealth. It can be modified to meet a different situation
but a Christian magistrate cannot swerve from its general equity
and substance. The Moral Law is usually, though not invariably,
identified with the Decalogue. It corresponds substantially to
the Law of Nature, originally given to Adam. It is not abolished
by the Gospel but regenerate Christians are freed from its bondage. The function of the Law is to discover and aggravate Sin
and by demonstrating that salvation is impossible under the
Law, to drive man to seek salvation in Christ. As Calvin puts it:
"The consequence then is, that all mankind are proved by the
law to be obnoxious to the curse and wrath of God; in order to
be saved from which they need deliverance from the power of
the law and emancipation from its servitude; not a carnal liberty
which would seduce us from obedience to the law, invite to all
kinds of licentiousness, break down the barriers of inordinate
desire and give the reins to every lawless passion; but a spiritual
liberty, which will console and elevate a distressed and dejected

conscience, showing it to be delivered from the curse and condemnation under which it was held by the law." (*Institutes, ed. cit.*, III, xvii, 1). Calvin's beliefs are also Milton's, but Milton is infinitely more humane than Calvin in his fervent insistence on the charity of the Gospel as opposed to the strict exactions of the Law.

Milton's lines are always compatible with accounts such as that of Elnathan Parr (*op. cit.*, pp. 271–310), of Wolleb-Ross (*op. cit.*, pp. 89–111), or of Andrew Willet (*Hexapla in Exodum*, London, 1633, pp. 264–69). But in spirit they are perhaps closer to John Smith (*op. cit.*, pp. 275–338) or to the near Antinomianism of Wolfgang Musculus (*Commonplaces of Christian Religion*, trans. John Man, London, 1578, pp. 278–83).

29. Parr, *op. cit.*, p. 226.
30. Roger Williams, *The Bloudy Tenet of Persecution* (London, 1644), pp. 206 ff.
31. Purchas, *Hakluytus Posthumous or Purchas his Pilgrimes* (Glasgow, 1905), p. 28.
32. Ussher, *op. cit.*, p. 201.
33. "A Treatise of Civil Power", *Works, ed. cit.*, vol. VI, p. 22.

NOTES TO "THE PROBLEM OF SATAN"

1. Raleigh, *Milton* (London, 1915), p. 133.
2. Especially Landor who, in a well-known passage, asserts that "there is neither wit nor truth however in saying that Satan is hero of the piece, unless, as is usually the case, he is the greatest hero who gives the widest sway to the worst passions". "Imaginary Conversations: Southey and Landor", *Works*, ed. C. G. Crump (London, 1891), vol. IV, p. 201. The comment is given to Southey.
3. *The English Poems of John Milton*, ed. Charles Williams (London, 1940), Intro. p. xv.
4. C. S. Lewis, *op. cit.*, pp. 92–100.
5. E. E. Stoll, "Give the Devil his Due", *R.E.S.*, XX (1944), pp. 108–24.
6. G. Rostrevor Hamilton, *Hero or Fool: A Study of Milton's Satan* (London, 1944).
7. Notably S. Musgrave's "Is the Devil an Ass?" (*R.E.S.*, XXI, 1945, pp. 302–15). I have not had access to Professor Waldock's "Mr. C. S. Lewis and *Paradise Lost*" (Australian English Association, 1943).
8. Calvin, *Institutes*, I, xiv, 13. Norton's translation.

NOTES TO pp. 90–109

9. Defoe, *The Political History of the Devil* (London, 1726), p. 52.
10. Addison in Todd, *ed. cit.*, vol. I, p. 302.
11. Addison, *loc. cit.*
12. Jeremy Taylor, *XXVIII Sermons* (London, 1651), p. 343.
13. Burton, *op. cit.*, pt. 3, mem. 1, sec. 4, subs. 2.
14. William Ames, *The Marrow of Sacred Divinity* (London, 1638), p. 324. Similarly Calvin comments on *Gen.* ii. 18: "Many think that celibacy conduces to their advantage, and, therefore, abstain from marriage, lest they should be miserable. . . . To these wicked suggestions of Satan, let the faithful learn to oppose this declaration of God, by which he ordains the conjugal life for man, not to his destruction but to his salvation." Ussher (*op. cit.*, p. 166) asserts that "man is naturally desirous of the society of women, and therefore . . . Munkeries, Nunneries and Hermitages are unnatural, and consequently ungodly". Gibbens (*op. cit.*, p. 89) talks of "this divelish doctrine of forbidding marriage" and claims that "The Apostle as one *foreseeing* this heresie in the Church, doth flatly cal it a *doctrine* of *divels*, and streightly chargeth all those to marrie, that have not received the gift of continencie".
15. See, e.g., *Paradise Lost*, VI, 398; VI, 742; VI, 767; VI, 801; VI, 882; X, 614. Defoe (*op. cit.*, p. 69) takes exception to this practice.
16. The ideas which Satan here misuses (IX, 99 ff.) remind us of Raphael's words to Adam (VIII, 91 ff.). At IX, 718 ff. Satan again misuses the idea that the sun, otherwise barren, is fruitful only as it serves the earth and man. This time he quotes in order to challenge (and significantly at the climax of the temptation) Raphael's opening words to Adam on degree (V, 469 ff.).

NOTES TO "THE STYLE OF PARADISE LOST"

1. R. D. Havens, *The Influence of Milton on English Poetry* (Camb., Mass., 1922), pp. 76–77 and p. 47.
2. The most striking evidence is in Milton's systematic varying of the position of the caesura. Thus according to J. W. Mackail (*The Springs of Helicon*, London, 1909, pp. 182–83) there are in the whole of *P.L.* less than twenty-five instances of the pause coming at the same point in the line for more than two lines consecutively.
3. According to J. C. Smith ("Feminine Endings in Milton's Blank Verse", *T.L.S.*, Dec. 5th, 1916, p. 1016) there are 93 such

L 161

endings in *Paradise Lost* of which 41 occur in the tenth book and 19 in *P.L.*, X, 867–95. Masson in his edition of Milton's Poems (London, 1882, vol. III, pp. 224–25) agrees that roughly 1 per cent of the lines in *P.L.* have feminine endings but counts "At least fifty-two" in *P.L.*, X. In Shakespeare the proportion is at its lowest in 1 *Henry IV* (5 per cent) and at its highest in *The Tempest* (35 per cent). (König, quoted Sir E. K. Chambers, *William Shakespeare. A Study of Facts and Problems*, Oxford, 1930, vol. II, p. 400).

4. According to T. H. Banks ("Miltonic Rhythm: A Study of the Relation of the Full Stops to the Rhythm of *Paradise Lost*", *P.M.L.A.*, XLII, 1927, pp. 140–45) 40 per cent of the full stops in *Paradise Lost* occur medially. "Full Stops" includes full stops, colons, periods, and question and exclamation marks when the latter occur at the end of a sentence. This extraordinarily high proportion of medial full stops tends to oppose the sentence to the line, and the tendency is strengthened by Milton's predilection for rhyming at the caesura. J. S. Diekhoff ("Rhyme in *Paradise Lost*", *P.M.L.A.*, XLIX, 1934, pp. 539–44) has counted nearly forty such instances in the first two books alone. By contrast there are only seventeen couplets in the whole epic and only a hundred and fourteen instances of rhymes separated by not more than two lines.

On my count 277 lines in *Paradise Lost*, or approximately 1 in 38, are wholly monosyllabic. The proportion is higher in dramatic blank verse and also in those portions of the epic consisting of dialogue or soliloquy. Of the 1,653 lines of this kind in the first four books, 70, or 1 in 24, are wholly monosyllabic. In the remaining 1,957 lines of narrative or description only 1 in 93 is wholly monosyllabic.

5. For a concise account of these characteristics see R. D. Havens, *op. cit.*, pp. 80–86 and J. H. Hanford, *A Milton Handbook* (New York, 1939), pp. 293–323. It is Milton's syntax rather than his vocabulary which is notable: a departure from the usual grammatical order is often accompanied by the insertion and amplification of subordinate elements which retard the completion of the sense. Such "suspension" undoubtedly contributes to the weight and solidity of Milton's style. It has been fully discussed by Gustav Hubener (*Die Stilistische Spannung in Milton's "Paradise Lost"*, Halle, 1913). But such analysis can be pushed too far and Mr. C. S. Lewis has done well to remind us (*op. cit.*, pp. 43–46) that Milton's syntax is emotional rather than logical. See also Hanford's discussion (*op. cit.*, pp. 299–301) of the poetical effect of some of Milton's syntactical ambiguities.

6. Walter Raleigh, *Milton* (London, 1915), p. 194.

7. C. S. Lewis, *op. cit.*, p. 45.
8. In my discussion of the Miltonic Simile I am greatly indebted to Mr. J. Whaler's four articles on the subject: "Grammatical Nexus of the Miltonic Simile", *J.E.G.P.*, XXXIII (1931), pp. 327–334; "The Compounding and Distribution of Simile in *Paradise Lost*", *M.P.*, XXVIII (1931), pp. 313–27; "The Miltonic Simile", *P.M.L.A.*, XLVI (1931), pp. 1034–1075, and "Animal Simile in *Paradise Lost*", *P.M.L.A.*, XLVII (1932), pp. 534–53.
9. *Antony and Cleopatra*, V, ii.
10. *Measure for Measure*, II, iv.
11. *Romeo and Juliet*, V, iii.
12. *Richard II*, V, ii.
13. *Essays of John Dryden. Selected and Edited by W. P. Ker* (Oxford, 1926), vol. I, pp. 226–27.
14. II *Henry IV*, Induction.
15. For discussion of the background see Theodore Spencer, *Death and Elizabethan Tragedy* (Camb., Mass., 1936).
16. The passage is discussed by Theodore Spencer, *op. cit.*, pp. 71–77. But Mr. Spencer is too concerned to treat the quotation as an assembly of stock ideas and so does not put his finger on the life of the metaphor.
17. James Whaler ("Animal Simile in *Paradise Lost*", p. 542) points out that there are only sixteen similes of more than two lines in the whole epic which are drawn from animal or plant life.
18. The ancestry of this simile is ably discussed by C. M. Bowra, *From Virgil to Milton* (London, 1945), pp. 240–41.
19. James Whaler, "The Miltonic Simile", p. 1034.
20. C. M. Bowra, *op. cit.*, p. 198.
21. W. Empson, *Some Versions of Pastoral* (London, 1935), pp. 149–91.
22. Cleanth Brooks, *Modern Poetry and the Tradition* (Chapel Hill, 1939), pp. 215–16.
23. John Bailey, *Milton* (London, 1915), p. 166.
24. E. E. Stoll, "Belial as an Example", *M.L.N.*, XLVIII (1933), pp. 419–27.
25. Mr. C. S. Lewis however makes too much of this self perpetuating tendency. "Once the diction has been established it works of itself. Almost anything the poet wants to say, has only to be turned into this orthodox and ready-made diction and it becomes poetry. 'Whatever Miss T. eats turns into Miss T.' The epic diction, as Goethe said, is 'a language which does your thinking and your poetizing for you.' " (*op. cit.*, p. 23). This is untrue and Milton would be a better poet if he did not sometimes write as if it were true.
26. According to my count, 2,140 lines of *Paradise Lost* are set in

Heaven. Yet in all these lines there is not a single complex or multiple simile, only one simile which involves a literary allusion, and only one place name, Biblical or Classical.

27. Professor Douglas Bush's analysis of *Paradise Lost*, I, 710 ff. (*"Paradise Lost" in Our Time*, Ithaca, 1945, pp. 98–100) should warn the Satanic School to read their texts more carefully. Milton's classical hell is rejected as it is described, and rejected by the poet as well as the Puritan. The truer criticism should be that nothing is put in its place. We may be convinced that it is wrong to reign in hell but we are not convinced (except as moralists) that it is right to serve in heaven.

INDEX TO PASSAGES FROM "PARADISE LOST"

GENERAL INDEX

Abel, 83
Abdiel, 31, 32, 102, 103
Adam, 12, 27, 28, 31, 44, 45,
    49, 59–60, 62, 63, 65–92, 97,
    99, 102
Adam Unparadiz'd, 78
Addison, Joseph, 58, 79, 94–5,
    147 n.
Agar, H., 158 n.
Ainsworth, Henry, 151 n.
Ainsworth, O. M., 11
Ambrose, St., 41
Ames, William, 99
Andrewes, Lancelot, 70, 149 n.,
    154 n., 156 n.
Angels, date of creation of, 33,
    40, 145 n.; date of fall of, 43;
    food, eating of by, 149 n.
Aquinas, St. Thomas, 43, 66,
    74–5, 145 n., 149–50 n., 157 n.
Areopagitica, 84
Ariosto, 123
Aubrey, John, 32
Augustine, St., 22, 43, 59, 67,
    141 n., 154 n.
Avitus, St., 41
Azazel, 47

Babington, Gervase, 156 n.,
    158 n.
Bailey, John, 79, 126, 147 n.
Baldwin, E. C., 10, 135 n.
Banks, T. H., 139 n., 162 n.
Barber, Rev. A. D., 22, 137–
    38 n., 140 n.
Barker, Arthur, 11, 142 n.
Basil, St., 41
Beaumont, Joseph, 155 n.
Beelzebub, 31

Belial, 13, 126
Bentley, Richard, 121
Bodin, Jean, 10
Boethius, 22
Bonaventure, St., 141 n., 148 n.
Bowra, C. M., 124
Bredvold, L., 10, 135 n.
Brooks, Cleanth, 124
Browne, Sir Thomas, 41, 67
Burton, Richard, 61, 81, 98,
    157 n.
Bush, Douglas, 164 n.

Caedmon, 40, 43, 155 n.
Cain, 83
Calvin, John, 17, 66, 75, 81, 94,
    145 n., 146 n., 150 n., 156 n.,
    158 n., 159–60 n., 161 n.
Campbell, L. B., 12, 158 n.
Ceres, 124
Charron, Pierre, 156 n.
Christ, 28, 30–31, 46, 47, 48,
    49, 57, 76, 83, 84, 90–91,
    106–7
Christian Liberty, 12, 18, 86,
    89, 159–60 n.
Chrysostom, St. John, 34
Comenius, Jan, 21, 137 n.
Conger, G. P., 158 n.
Copernican System, 65, 152–
    53 n.
Cowley, Abraham, 54–55, 122
Cowper, William, 146 n.
Crashaw, Richard, 146 n.
Curry, Walter Clyde, 12, 137 n.,
    150 n.

Danaeus, Lambertus, 141 n.
Daniel, Samuel, 110

167

PRINTED IN GREAT BRITAIN BY ROBERT MACLEHOSE AND CO. LTD.
THE UNIVERSITY PRESS, GLASGOW